ECHOES FROM
A MASON'S JOURNEY

Assorted Commentaries from a Mason on a Quest

PAST MASTER WILLIAM H. BOYD

PAST MASTER WILLIAM H. BOYD
Perfect Ashlar Publishing
perfectashlarpublishing@gmail.com
Universal City, TX

Printed Worldwide
First Printing 2025
First Edition 2025

10 9 8 7 6 5 4 3 2 1

Interior Book Design by Walt's Book Design
www.waltsbookdesign.com

For ordering information, please visit Perfect Ashlar Publishing's website at:
www.PerfectAshlarPublishing.com

ECHOES FROM
A MASON'S JOURNEY

TABLE OF CONTENTS

INTRODUCTION 1

THE QUEST FOR MASONRY 3

    SEIZE YOUR JOURNEY 4

    PICTURE THIS! 7

    STAND IN THE BREACH 12

    LESSONS FROM TUN TAVERN 17

    RETURN TO TUN TAVERN 20

    WORKING TOOLS OF A WORSHIPFUL MASTER 28

    CHASING TITLES, OR LEVELING UP? 32

    "ON TIME" & "MASONRY IN A CHANGING CULTURE – A FOLLOW-UP" 36

    CATECHISMS AND FLOORWORK 41

IN AND ABOUT THE LODGE 47

    SHOULD I BELONG TO TWO LODGES? 48

    THE SEAT IN THE EAST - VIRTUES OF A MASTER 50

    WHO COULD LOVE THE CEREMONIAL "READING OF THE MINUTES"? 55

    MENTORING IN MASONRY 59

    MENTORING ON THE FLY 64

    BASIC MILITARY TRAINING – OR BASIC MASONIC TRAINING? 67

    A LETTER TO MY BROTHER 73

SYMBOLISM AND ALLEGORY 79

    TRAVELING GATE-TO-GATE 80

    GATE-TO-GATE (A TRIBUTE) 83

    WAIT... MASONRY EXPECTS ME TO DO MATH? 87

ABOUT THE AUTHOR 93

A NOTE TO THE READER 95

OTHER BOOKS BY PERFECT ASHLAR PUBLISHING 97

INTRODUCTION

This book is a collection of some of my blog posts that – as of this printing – are posted and reside on my website ("*A Mason's Journey*"). Web postings are not forever; websites come and go, and when they go, they take their content with them unless that content is captured in some fashion for posterity. This is the purpose of this particular collection – to preserve my favorite blog posts for posterity, just in case there is interest or a need for them in the future.

In the course of my brief writing career, I've dabbled in articles, blog posts, educational materials, non-fiction books, and of course, my fictional "*Noah*" series. After two years of self-publishing my nonfiction works in various forms, I conducted an experiment in which I used a short, fictional story to convey my ideas about the relationship between our "masonic west gate" and the "Pearly Gate." That short story evolved into a book, and then that book became "Noah's Quest." Finally, "Noah's Quest" became my "Noah" series, where I explored and tested all my ideas and beliefs about masonry through topical challenges for my fictional protagonist, Noah Lewis. Let there be no doubt whatsoever that every single test and trial that Noah Lewis endured throughout his quest originated from one (and sometimes more) of my web articles and blog posts.

I've decided to preserve my favorite blog posts for current and future brothers in masonry, should there be a desire or some level of curiosity. I've organized the posts into three sections according to specific themes: general Masonic ideas, lodge administration (also known as "In and About the Lodge"), and my esoteric and symbolic perspectives on the craft. I will also include a narrative explanation for some of these posts to share my thoughts on how and why they came to be, or perhaps some other relevant bit of trivia. In my *"Noah"* series, I created a personal working tool I call the *"Backstage Pass"* to take a reader behind the scenes and explain my thinking on specific details or to highlight and reinforce the importance of others, and I will use this tool for those narrative explanations.

For those who have read these posts, you may notice that I have provided some editorial "cleanup" in the content since its original publication online. For those who have not read these yet, I hope they provide you with some food for thought or perhaps even inspire you in some way as you travel your unique path. Let your journey be energized by this powerful question: *"What if"*?

THE QUEST FOR MASONRY

SEIZE YOUR JOURNEY

December 17, 2021

BACKSTAGE PASS: An oldie but a goody to be sure! This was very early in my writing career, and I had not yet developed a sound "write-edit-polish-publish" process. I took this opportunity to refine the edges, and you will notice some minor differences between this item and the original post. This still resonates with me today as deeply as it did when I originally posted it, and I still offer this advice to my brothers and friends!

**

Carpe iter tuum! You may recognize this more easily in English: "*seize your journey*"! I am a strong advocate of one taking charge of their journey or destiny and plowing ahead, clearing their path as they go. What prompts me to address this topic with my keyboard? The answer is simple: reading, listening, and hearing what is being discussed and pondered among some of our brethren.

I frequently see and hear brothers seeking advice and guidance on their next masonic step, what masonic orders to join, or perhaps where to devote their energies and labors; to be honest, I am all in on seeking the opinions and experiences of brethren who have advanced in their journeys and who are pursuing their masonic interests. Our brothers are out there, living the "masonic life" and learning about masonry, other orders, history, and ritual. They are our best resources for information we can use to make our own decisions on what's next and where our paths should go.

I would caution a brother, however, about the potential for one to, in essence, surrender their journey or control over their journey to others based on the experiences and opinions of the more experienced brothers. Brethren, I implore you to seek out the advice of others, but please make your final decisions based on your interests and desires. Once you change your mind on a decision about your next step based on what a brother advises, or when you accept what you believe to be a common opinion held by what you *presume* is a majority of brothers, you have in essence surrendered that decision to that brother or group and, therefore, you also have surrendered control over that part of your journey to others.

I cannot emphasize too strongly the importance of what I am about to say; *opinions and experiences of brothers is crucial in helping a mason make well-informed decisions about their masonic futures, but one should never make such a personal decision based on things he might hear or read on social media or, worse, based on beliefs he might consider to be widely held.* An example I recently discovered had a brother pondering a Masonic organization that he was particularly interested in and drawn to. Still, he was hesitating because he believed that the popular opinion of many brothers was that it was not a good idea or "*not right*" for him. This brother turned to social media for input and thoughts not only of brothers, but those who populate online masonic forums, but may not be masons or even have the best interest of masonry in mind. I got the sense this brother might actually decide against joining the organization based on feedback from potentially hundreds of online "*users*" he had never met. This, to me, is *the* classic example of surrendering your journey to others – worse, it is surrendering it to people who don't know you.

The trick, my brothers, is to gather your information from those whom you know and trust, evaluate their advice and opinions, and weigh that information against your interests and *then* make your *own* decision based on what they have told you and what you know to be best for you.

For new master masons, this is a tricky endeavor. There will be many opinions and experiences from many brothers, and the new mason will have little or *no* frame of reference. However, this is also an opportunity for the new brother to examine his own expectations and hopes for his Masonic future and acknowledge them. This can help him learn and improve his ability to identify his natural instincts, trust them, and act on them. This will be a lifelong lesson reinforced frequently throughout his journey and will serve him well in his many Masonic and non-Masonic endeavors. Well-informed decision-making is a critical life skill that a man requires to be successful, but, in the end, it might remain dormant in a man who makes a lifelong habit of surrendering his decisions to others or to popular opinions.

Brethren, it is *your* journey! Good brothers will come and go, and each will bring their own experiences and advice – but their opinions are based on *their* journey! Social media users may or may not actually be masons, so what is their advice actually worth? None of these good brothers or social media users are walking your path or pursuing your interests and goals, so why would you, why would *we* surrender our decisions to them? My brother, Carpe iter tuum! Seize <u>your</u> journey!

S&F

Bro. Bill

PICTURE THIS!

Publishing EA & FC Names and Pictures

February 15, 2022

BACKSTAGE PASS: This is a frequent topic of discussion – whether to celebrate our Entered Apprentices and Fellowcrafts when they reach each masonic milestone, or to wait until they reach the ultimate goal when they are officially raised to the sublime degree of a master mason. I took my keyboard in hand and rattled out my thoughts in the following article, and they remain essentially unchanged to this day.

⋆⋆

As I wait for my next paper to come back from peer review, this seems to be a good time to squeeze in another topic that has been bubbling at or just under the surface for some time, but broke through to the surface this year within the jurisdiction of the Grand Lodge of Texas. The issue I am referring to is the publication of pictures of our Entered Apprentices (EA) and Fellowcrafts (FC), especially immediately after they receive their degrees.

This question and open discussion arose again through a resolution submitted for consideration at the Annual Communication of the Grand Lodge of Texas this January in Waco. The resolution would have extended the existing ban on publishing the names of petitioners and candidates to include their pictures, especially on social media. Had it passed, it would have prohibited the publishing of the name and photo of a new EA or FC anywhere, in any publication. The resolution failed, but it was probably not due to the substance of the question. It likely failed due to the committee's report, which informed Grand West that if the resolution were adopted as written, it would prohibit entering the names of EAs and FCs into our Grand Lodge database, called "Grand View". That's just not logical or practical, so the resolution failed on the ballot, likely due primarily to the poor construction and precision of its wording.

I've had this discussion with several brothers, both in the past and again more recently, as a result of the failed resolution. I do not presume my view to be the "*correct*" view, or even a better view than any other brother's view. We all have our opinions on this subject, and I merely seek to offer mine here, in this forum, for consideration by those who have already decided one way or another or who may still be undecided.

As you may have guessed or suspected, I oppose publishing the name and/or picture of any EA or FC candidate. Why do I oppose the idea of publishing the names and pictures of candidates? Obviously, I'm old and "*clinging to the ways of the past*". Yes, that may be true, but humor aside, my "*traditionalist*" side naturally falls into the opposition camp, but I do have what I think are more modern and practical reasons, which I will list:

First, a candidate's primary aspiration should and *must* be to complete his work and to be raised to the sublime degree of a master mason. We stress throughout his time as both EA and FC that there is nothing higher, no better status, than that of Master Mason, and once he achieves that, he will earn his full and rightful recognition. Yet, we have, within the last generation or two of masons, begun celebrating every advancement and achievement as major and worthy of celebration. It is my opinion that completing your EA and FC degrees and catechisms are expected and required, so why do we put them on par with the joy and reward of achieving the significant masonic milestone of being raised? Might this be the masonic form of the "*participation trophy*", ultimately cheapening the celebration after a new master's raising?

Second, we celebrate a man completing merely the first part of his initiation, and yet we still see many men drift off, failing to complete any other part of their work. These men, who have drifted off, have, in many cases, received the same celebration and recognition as those who will go on to complete all their work. In my mind, celebration and public recognition should be reserved for those who complete their tasks and attain the desirable and sublime degree of a master mason.

Third, by making grand public announcements of achievement at each of the three Masonic degree levels, we dilute the value, importance, and impressiveness of the achievement of being raised, lowering its stature to that of being equal to that of EAs and FCs. Should the accomplishment of being raised be no different than that of being initiated in the public's eye?

Fourth, by publishing pictures of our EAs and FCs, do we draw men who may merely be seeking similar public recognition without giving much serious consideration to the work necessary to achieve the third and most important degree? How many men might we have lost along the way because they were lured in by pictures of their friends and acquaintances being publicly hailed, yet have given no thought to the serious work necessary behind the scenes to advance, and discover instead it's not to their liking? Are our pictorial celebrations of initiations and passings portraying a skewed or inaccurate picture for those who are merely curious about masonry? I don't claim to know, but I am intrigued by the question itself, and it is something I do think about.

Fifth, imagine non-masons seeing our EAs and FCs' pictures on their social media news feeds and then asking them questions about what masonry is and how it works. What kind of answers can you imagine them providing? When a non-mason relative asks the EA, "So tell me about your initiation," or "Tell *me, what do masons do*?". How prepared is an EA to field those questions? And you know the EA and FC will eventually be told, maybe after posting his EA picture, that "*you haven't gone high enough yet to learn about the dark side of masonry*". Why put the EA in the position to be so challenged by his non-masonic friends and relatives? I believe this is one of the important reasons we have traditionally shielded the names of candidates from the public until after they are raised to the sublime degree.

Finally, on a lesser note, how many men who were merely curious about masonry, paid their degree fee, tried it out, and then walked away are now out there boasting "*I'm a mason, see, here's the picture of when I was initiated*"? How many might use this as their proof of credibility to speak and write about masonry - *for or against* - while flaunting their picture and saying, "See, *I know what I'm talking about, I'm a mason, so I am fully qualified to write about masonry and what it is.*" I personally don't see any benefit in providing a picture of an EA (or FC) surrounded by brothers that a man with less-than-honorable intentions might then use to establish a false credibility among those supporting his nefarious or bitter intentions.

Yes, I do suffer from "*old think*" on this matter. However, the discussion will continue, and brothers will weigh in. In Texas, we may even use the recent ballot as a way forward to allow and endorse the posting of EA and FC pictures.

If that is how this unfolds, then so be it, and I am fully capable of moving forward with our Grand Lodge decisions. I will likely remain personally opposed for the reasons I've stated here, but I remain open-minded. Like my paper and position on alcohol at the lodge, I can and might be convinced to change my mind. However, I have not yet heard the argument that would sway me, but I am listening.

STAND IN THE BREACH

January 23, 2023

BACKSTAGE PASS: This one came about as my frustration over continuous and pointless (actionless) complaining that seemed to be spreading among the brethren. I frequently hear complaints, but I see very few brothers who are ultimately moved to action. You will find that I edited this one significantly for grammar and readability.

**

Who will stand in the defense of masonry? Who will stand in the breach? This question arises from many discussions I've had since I started researching, writing, and publishing articles and books. It is now bubbling around in my head, and it will become a Blog Post, then it will become an article, and perhaps I will work it into a book in the near future. The real question is this: "*When push comes to shove, who among us will fight for our craft through tough love, pointed and very direct masonic education, strict petition investigations, and the expectation and application of very high standards in our lodges and among our brothers*"?

Here is a test that each of you can do, and that I have been doing for almost four years now. Randomly ask brothers you know this question: "*What do you think is wrong with masonry today*?". It's a simple question, and the answers will reflect the opinion(s) of those whom you ask.

Here are the essentials to consider once you begin your survey:

First, how many brothers respond with two or more issues that really bug them? Inversely, how many love everything about the craft exactly as it is?

Second, of the answers you receive, how many of the problems or issues are you personally already familiar with and perhaps agree with?

Third, after you have asked the number of brothers you have selected, how many different issues surfaced as things that bother your brothers?

As in any family, there are always small issues that members either dislike or may even drive them a little bit crazy. However, because they are a true family, they find their own way to address or cope with the problem personally. Some individuals ignore the problems, perhaps assuming that there are things they themselves do that drive others in the family crazy. Others, however, will address the issues head-on with the family member at the center of the problem. Strong, healthy families work through these types of problems and move forward.

Unfortunately, in some families, members ignore problems and avoid confrontations simply - *as they believe* – to avoid bigger problems. I think we all know that problems ignored will eventually demand attention and even action; it's just a matter of when and how much damage is done when the dam bursts.

When you asked your brothers what things bother them about the fraternity, did any indicate what, if anything, they had done to address the problem or problems? If any of the issues were the same as any of the ones that you yourself find to be causing problems or contention among your brothers, what have *you* done to address the problems?

"Problems ignored will eventually demand attention and even action; it's just a matter of when, and how much damage is done when the dam bursts".

If you informally sampled the thoughts of five or six brothers and were surprised to find that there are eight or nine, or perhaps even more issues on the minds of brothers in your lodge, yet no one is moving to address or correct them, at least some of those problems will eventually demand attention. Is it your hope that when that happens, it is someone else's job to deal with it? Do you hope you don't get pulled into the unpleasant vortex that might emerge as the wheels come off? Or perhaps you may feel that yes, you understand the problems and issues, but they simply aren't your problems to address.

Let's go one more step. Suppose 15 or 20 brothers you know from your lodge and perhaps other lodges as well all have four or five things that really bother them about the craft, and everyone is sitting back, waiting for someone else to address them.

Who will stand in defense of the craft and who will stand in the breach when the winds start to blow?

Who will take an issue they have with masonry and try to fix it? Who will say to themselves, *"this makes no sense, and I will do my best to improve it!!"*?

Will YOU work in the quarry to improve our fraternal temple? Will you write a resolution to improve that article in the law book you really hate? Will you research and design an educational program to teach brothers something they need to know about the craft that they may have never seen or been taught? Will you tell a brother that it's highly distracting and impolite to talk on the sideline during a meeting or, even worse, during a degree?

My brothers, if you run that little test where you ask several brothers what they don't like about masonry or our fraternity, don't stop there - think about the answers and force yourself to understand what those answers mean, and if you find you agree with others about those certain issues or problems, then step up and into the breach! *LEAD!* Acknowledge the things that impact the fraternity, then take action to address them.

Masonry only works to improve a man when a man actively engages with our common and unifying system of morality. Bored in the lodge? Start a club. Think there are better options and ways to take care of the lodge? Volunteer to be on or even to lead a committee! Do you think things could run better? Volunteer for the line and address your ideas and suggestions with the weight of an officer of the lodge. Do you have ideas to explain or improve the craft? Write an article, a blog, *or a book*! Engage with the lodge and explore masonry to make it work for you and your lodge!

I will offer one word of recommendation or caution. When you take on a problem or an issue, keep your mind and your eyes open! Do not enter the battle under the assumption that you already know everything about the issue - be prepared to learn. You may find out there are other factors at play that you knew nothing about. If this occurs, learn everything you can about the entire issue and *all* the factors, and then share that information with your brothers who probably do not have the additional knowledge you have learned. Educate and share the light with your brothers!

Are we not taught, and do we not teach, that masonry is a system designed in such a way as to make good men better? A man who sees a problem and then thinks it through, and then proposes a solution, ultimately makes himself and the craft better! Leadership, problem-solving, motivating those around you, and perhaps public speaking are all aspects you might improve in yourself while you also improve your lodge and the fraternity!

My brothers, I see a clear choice - sit around, grumble about things that bother us and make those around us miserable too, or take advantage of the opportunities afforded us through masonry and make ourselves, our lodges, and our craft, a better fraternity for all of us! Any man from Entered Apprentice to Master Mason can spot a problem, but leaders go further and address the problems they identify. Stand in the breach!

Travel with purpose, my brothers!

Bro. Bill

LESSONS FROM TUN TAVERN

November 11, 2023

BACKSTAGE PASS: This post actually spurred one of my most controversial blog posts ("*Return to Tun Tavern*"), which follows. While this post addresses our membership numbers in the context of other organizations, it also sets the stage for my extraordinary suggestion in the next post to address our perceived shortfall in new members. As in the other posts, I have edited this somewhat for grammar and punctuation.

**

As we ponder and extend our appreciation to our generations of military veterans on this Veteran's Day, let's look at a lesson we might take away from this year's annual tribute: what can we learn that might help our fraternity?

I wrote last year in my article "*Freemasonry in a Changing Culture*"[1] about membership trends in masonry versus the trends of various fraternal organizations that are typically prominent in our many communities, particularly veterans' organizations such as The American Legion and the Veterans of Foreign Wars of the United States. In my research, I discovered that our fraternity is suffering in a similar manner from low "recruiting" numbers and declining membership totals.

---

[1] "*Freemasonry in a Changing Culture*" was published in my book "*Guard Well Our Craft*" in 2022 by Perfect Ashlar Publishing. It is found on pages 49 through 106 in the Amazon paperback edition.

In fact, because those organizations actively and openly recruit and are also suffering similar effects from recent generations who seem disinclined to join, it *may* be that they are in *worse shape* than we believe our own fraternity to be in.

Perhaps on this Veteran's Day of 2023, there is a shimmer of light for us. As we consider our armed forces in terms of those who have served, and as we look at the recruiting trends throughout the military today, we find a growing crisis in recruiting similar to what we find in veterans' organizations, our services are also failing to meet their annual recruiting goals with one exception – *the United States Marine Corps.*

Masonic membership appears to be declining, college dropout rates are soaring, fraternal organizations are in the midst of a nationwide recruiting crisis, and the USMC is meeting its recruiting goals – without lowering standards and while still rejecting *the unqualified.*

What are we to make of this? Is it a fluke? Not likely. The Marine Corps is 248 years old this year, and it's still going strong. What might this mean for us? Here's what I think: I believe it's their very exclusivity and demanding entrance standards that make them the most desirable of our armed services. They are open about their standards, and they boast in their public recruiting campaigns that not everyone can make it through the door. Those that do will find it challenging, tough, and that it will be impossible for many to even complete boot camp and claim the title United States Marine.

What do you suppose they know that we might be missing, and what lessons might we learn from Tun Tavern? Let us ponder these questions and, while we do, let's wish a Happy Birthday to the United States Marine Corps and thank them for their ideals and their instinctive and traditional leadership that prohibits them from lowering their standards in the face of swirling societal and cultural forces that seem to be re-making our country in front of our eyes.

Travel on my brothers!

RETURN TO TUN TAVERN

November 12, 2023

BACKSTAGE PASS: This is essentially a "Part Two" to the previous piece, "*Lessons from Tun Tavern*". As soon as I posted that original blog post, my mind began wrestling with the "*so what*" question; "*so what*" if the Marine Corps is able to consistently meet its annual recruiting goals, even when virtually every other military service and veteran organization is failing to? What could that mean for masonry? I worked on a piece where I both analyzed and explained the comparison, tied it to our Masonic membership issue, and then proposed a somewhat outlandish idea to address our fraternal member rolls. Let us "return to Tun Tavern" and examine my idea. Again, I have done some minor editing for clarity, grammar, and punctuation.

**

I wrote a blog post on Veterans Day about our membership struggles in masonry compared to the membership issues facing other military, fraternal, veteran, and social organizations. I pointed out that among all the examples (military services, college fraternities, veterans' organizations, etc.), the United States Marine Corps (USMC) stands out, far ahead of all others in both recruiting and retention. Among them, only the Marines have maintained their original recruiting and induction standards, their original training standards, and their expected high performance and strict behavioral standards while also still enjoying a high level of interest and desire among prospective recruits. I left off by posing one question for us, for our fraternity to consider: "What do you suppose they know that we might be missing, and what lessons might we learn from Tun Tavern?"

Let us return briefly to Tun Tavern, home of the USMC and, by the way, also recognized since the 1700s as the seat of Masonic teachings in America at the time. The tavern hosted the inaugural conference of the American Freemasonic order as well as the election of the first Grand Master of the Grand Lodge of Pennsylvania in 1732. I think with credentials such as these, it is entirely appropriate to look there-to our roots-as we ponder the future of our masonic order.

After I posted *"Lessons from Tun Tavern"*, something nagged me for several hours before I was able to see *"it"* take shape and become clear. What emerged was a question that we might pose, at least rhetorically, to initiate some serious thought and an effective conversation about the future of Masonic membership standards and the state of our lodges as we enter that future.

I pose this simple, though highly controversial and seemingly unserious, question for your thoughtful consideration and to stimulate real and substantive discussions:

"What would your lodge do and how would it impact our fraternity if we passed a resolution at the next Grand Communication that limited our lodges - all lodges - to three candidate initiations (three Entered Apprentices) per masonic year?"

Remember the context in which this question was born - the USMC has a cap or limit on how many recruits they are allowed to induct into the service each year. They administer various qualification tests such as the Armed Services Vocational Aptitude Battery, they do investigative criminal background checks on each candidate, they publicly boast about how hard it is to join and then they brag about how hard it is to complete boot camp after joining; yet in spite of all of that they *still* have a waiting list each year for men and women who want to join and become one of the proud and one of the few.

While it might seem outrageous to suggest capping initiations at three per year per lodge, *and perhaps it is*, I ask you to play the scenario out in your mind as a way of provoking ideas and discussions about our existing membership concerns. Some lodges today regularly initiate many new EAs every year, while some probably struggle to initiate two or three, so what would the effect of such a new rule be?

It is worth pointing out that throughout our jurisdiction, retention is just as significant a concern as initiating new members, and we are seeing some troubling numbers for those failing to complete their EA and FC work; is there something that might address this buried within the discussion of my seemingly preposterous suggestion of capping the number of EAs?

As I worked my way through the counterintuitive idea of limiting our initiations and considered the various effects of such a law, I realized that some companion changes to our law book and procedures might be necessary to make this work on a practical basis. To advance this exercise, here is a list of some additional changes I think we would have to make to implement such a cap on membership and generate positive effects across the state:

1. Cap all lodges at three EA initiations per masonic year

2. Remove the requirement to ballot on a petition within 30 days - change it to say instead that all petitions formally accepted and read in lodge must be balloted at a Stated Meeting not later than the final Stated Meeting of the masonic year - this would allow lodges to establish longer and more effective "*getting to know you*" timelines where they can get to know potential petitioners and complete more effective and very thorough investigations

3. Allow lodges to appoint a committee and begin investigations upon receipt of the petition instead of waiting until after it is read in lodge; this could be done at a called meeting

4. Allow a lodge to reject a petition out of hand "*without prejudice*" and without a formal reading in an open lodge - a lodge might identify their three desired candidates early in the year and would then be allowed to return any further petitions to those additional prospective petitioners without prejudice allowing them to legally petition any other lodge and answer truthfully that they have not previously petitioned any other lodge[2]

---

[2] In this new situation, a petition could either be "returned without prejudice" as described, or balloted and rejected "with prejudice" which would require a petitioner to acknowledge petitioning the lodge if they ever petition another lodge in the future.

Now, having set some practical conditions, let's proceed with this exercise and see what we might discover. Lodges with high initiation rates would be the first ones to feel the effects of a "three initiation" cap, so let's begin our exploration there.

If your lodge traditionally initiates more than three EAs per year and you suddenly found your lodge capped at three, what adjustments would you have to make? If you have three "slots" and eight prospective candidates interested in petitioning your lodge for the degrees, how do you identify the three best candidates? This is where I think the other proposed changes will work in favor of the lodges. Lodges in the situation I've described could accept the petitions of all eight and immediately begin their investigations while still withholding the formal ballot in the lodge. The lodge can also set a formal "getting to know you" period where the eight prospective candidates might attend functions, socialize with lodge members, and volunteer time and labor to assist the lodge with programs and chores as a way of demonstrating not only their seriousness, but their intent to be active in lodge. Imagine having eight prospective candidates that you have been observing for nine months and some of them are obviously eager to be part of the lodge while the others perhaps only attend to share meals and socialize. In my theoretical scenario, this lodge could simply return the unread petitions to the *"less-than-eager"* *prospects and forward the petitions and investigative reports of the serious* *contenders to the Secretary to be balloted in the* lodge.

Can I prove that the prospective candidates selected in this example would be hard charging brothers who are guaranteed to finish their work and be active in lodge? No, I can't say that with one hundred percent certainty, but over the span of nine or ten months where we watch and interact with all of the prospective candidates, I think we would be able to say that we accepted the petitions from those that seemed *most likely* to finish their work and become active. Our three "EA slots" for this year would now be filled by petitioners that we believe are likely to meet our expectations and are most likely to be successful in masonry. Think of it in the context of our Tun Tavern ancestors; Marine recruiters will interview prospective recruits and, if they select them, they'll tell the prospect to use the time before he is inducted and takes his oath of office to get ready physically and mentally for the challenges that lay ahead. A more or less formal "*getting-to-know-you*" period in the lodges might allow the brethren to go through a similar process in getting their prospective petitioners ready for their initiation and obligation.

For lodges that are typically under the proposed three-EA cap every year, we might be safe in speculating that men that can't get initiated into lodges that are "capped out" for the year *might* then visit and ask to petition at some of these smaller lodges and provide a boost to those membership rolls. I freely admit this is less than ideal because a man's participation and attendance is always heavily impacted by the distance he has to travel to lodge, but with an extended "*getting-to-know-you*" period coupled with the new option to investigate early while delaying the ballot, it might be possible for those smaller lodges to identify those who are impacted by time, distance, and life's conflicts, or even those who may be less-than-serious about their intentions to become a mason before they are initiated. These smaller lodges have the same options to return a petition without prejudice and preserve one of their three precious EA slots for the year.

It is quite possible that in a new environment of capped EA slots across the state, many small lodges would see an uptick in visits by prospective petitioners in search of lodges with uncommitted EA slots and those lodges might then also enjoy being in a position to select their three EAs from a newly expanded pool of interested prospects.

So, what is the basis for this little exercise? Why should we even bother consider capping membership when our top concern for the future of masonry is our widely held perception that our member rolls are shrinking? Perhaps we should consider the allure of an organization that is only available to the few, the dedicated, and the serious in the same fashion as our fellow Tun Tavern ancestors. There is something enticing about an organization that says, "we don't take just anyone, and we expect and demand much from those we do select". As Thomas Paine once said: "*that which we obtain too cheaply we esteem too lightly*".

I am frequently accused of - *and I will admit to* - being resistant to change (for the sake of change). But I am not reflexively resistant to all changes - if they make sense for the fraternity and do not disrupt or alter the intent of our masonic craft and ritual(s). The premise of this particular thought exercise is obviously to consider a change - *however unrealistic* - that might provide one way to raise our bar, raise our standards, and become much more selective in who we accept as masons among us, identifying and focusing on those most likely to finish their degree work and contribute to their lodges. Yes, we might become smaller, but perhaps our bonds and the fraternity will grow stronger!

On the other hand it is also possible that strengthening our reputation as an organization of the few, select men of quality and impeccable reputations and as one that touts a quiet mystique might renew a societal curiosity in masonry that might ultimately increase our membership numbers over time and do so by attracting those men most likely to be successful and productive in the fraternity and in our communities and are willing to *prove it* through their actions during the time their petitions are under consideration.

Two organizations, both with roots in Tun Tavern and both imbued with the principles and beliefs necessary to go forward to found, build, fight for, and protect our great nation. One of these organizations continues marching resolutely forward today, accepting only the best while leaving others wanting, waiting, and wishing for an opportunity; the other questions its membership trends and its very future. I ask again, what might we learn from our ancestors of Tun Tavern?

WORKING TOOLS OF A WORSHIPFUL MASTER

December 3, 2023

BACKSTAGE PASS: This post came about one night after a lengthy philosophical discussion with a brother about working tools. Somewhere in our back-and-forth, one of us uttered the words "seems like the Worshipful Master should have working tools," and it essentially brought the discussion to a halt. After a moment or two, we both agreed that if our Entered Apprentices, Fellowcrafts, and Master Masons had working tools, then a Worshipful Master certainly needed them as well. The result of that discussion follows, and, like the others, it has been edited for clarity, grammar, and punctuation so it appears slightly changed from the original post.

✶✶

What are the Working Tools of a Worshipful Master? Does the Worshipful Master even need Working Tools? Why does he need them? All very good questions and the answer, I believe, is critical to the success and perhaps even the survival of our lodges.

We are told of the importance of the Worshipful Master in various programs and rituals. We learn that he holds the symbolic leadership position among the various lights that guide the lodge in its duties and ritual. We also understand his duty to set the craft to labor and provide instruction on the duties required for the successful operation of the lodge. And finally, we are reminded every year of the Worshipful

Master's lengthy list of responsibilities when we attend our annual Installation of Officers and listen while he is both obligated and charged by the Installing Master. It is clear that a man and a brother coming into the position of Worshipful Master could use his own working tools to assist in his labors on behalf of the lodge.

I believe that the proper working tools of a Worshipful Master should be the gavel and the hat. Like all of the other working tools we gather as we traverse the paths of our respective journeys, these working tools would necessarily symbolize something, right?

As operative masons, our Worshipful Masters employ the gavel and hat as physical and visual representations of their governance and authority over and within the lodge. As the gavel calls the craft to order, it also maintains protocols, decorum, and manners among the brethren. The hat serves as a visual representation of the Worshipful Master's authority, rallying us to unite under his leadership and in support of his directions and decisions.

But as speculative masons, we might see them together as representing "*Harmony, Vision, and Unity*" which might be interpreted thusly:

Where the Worshipful Master ensures that *harmony* exists, we are able to labor together in good cheer and high spirit in support of our lodges and of each other, sharing the demands of our efforts and together enjoying the fruits resulting from our mutual labors.

When the Worshipful Master presents his vision for our lodge, we are called to work in unison, mindful of the lodge's needs and our brothers' needs, to complete our necessary tasks and reach a common goal, a goal that has been described but remains to be attained.

And when there is adequate communication from the Worshipful Master to the craft, *unity* can follow. We can learn our tasks and expectations, and we are afforded due opportunities to join in the mutual labors of our brethren, ultimately reaping the spiritual rewards that come from investing our precious time and unified efforts in our lodge with our brothers.

My objective with this offering is to shine some informative light on what I believe are the three principle responsibilities of the Worshipful Master in his presiding year: *ensure harmony in and about the lodge,* where harmony prevails brotherly love can follow; *communicate a unifying vision* to harness the energy and labors of the brethren and effectively focus them on a common objective or goal; and finally, to communicate with his members - all of his members. The brethren cannot help and cannot unify as one band of brothers if they don't know where the Worshipful Master is taking the lodge and what he needs the brethren to do to get there; lodges generally do *not* demise because they share *too much* information with its members; get the word out, make every brother feel as if he is an integral part of an extended but unified family!

I offer these thoughts, and I implore our future Worshipful Masters to at least consider these working tools and adopt—or adapt—them. You might adopt them as I have described them here, or perhaps you might find a useful adaptation that better fits your lodge and circumstance; in either case, it is always worthwhile organizing your thoughts and your labors before trying to organize those of your lodge and your brothers!

Labor on my worthy brothers - and let's put *all* of our Working Tools to use!

-BroBill

CHASING TITLES, OR LEVELING UP?

December 15, 2023

BACKSTAGE PASS: Sometimes I watch debates – okay, arguments – explode on social media and I become hooked, following each post, each reply closely. These virtual debates can erupt without notice, seemingly out of nowhere, and can last for days. In most cases, I don't necessarily pick a side that I believe in or support and then mentally root for those who also agree; instead, I try to determine which side or position is well-supported by facts, and whether either side is mounting merely an emotional argument. Then I look to see if the various participants are covering all of the various aspects of the question or position, and if anyone has added anything I had not thought of or considered. Normally, by the time they figure all of this out, the debate has settled, and the various participants have (virtually) wandered off. Sometimes, important new information comes out, but often emotions get ruffled, and the participants leave in a huff. The following post arose from one of these online debates that I followed for several days, which ultimately ended with no significant shift in anyone's opinion and no new facts for consideration. This post presents my thoughts on the topic, which I invite readers to ponder as they see fit. I have revised the article with some minor editing to improve readability, grammar, and punctuation.

⁎⁎

I take the keyboard in hand to examine a topic that comes up fairly regularly on social media - "I have no respect for someone who chases titles," or "I can't take 'title chasers' seriously." I always find this subject particularly curious, coming from brothers who are theoretically on a journey to make themselves better. I need to be up front with my record, which I am sure would fall into this pejorative "title chaser" category that seems to be firmly defined by those who have never met me. I have presided over several bodies, and I have served as a District Deputy in two bodies (details are all in my bio on my website), attributes that I suppose might define me as one of these elusive "title chasers".

Initially, and for several years, I always reacted to these discussions as being curious and somewhat insulting - particularly when they were discussed broadly and without defining who or what titles they were referring to. It struck me as presumptive (at best) to assume that those selected for various positions and titles "*chased*" that accolade in some fashion and that the title itself is important to some particular brothers. I am not so naive as to believe that there are no brothers actively seeking offices and titles; I'm sure there are. However, that fact does not negate my thoughts, which I will share hereafter.

After some time and some deeper reflection on this question of "chasing titles", I have embraced a new view or a new opinion on this matter. We all theoretically approach our west gate with a goal of making ourselves better men, according to the promise of our primary craft selling point. Some men will enter our world to mix and socialize in a group for the first time ever. Perhaps they feel awkward, maybe even embarrassed at their short "*life's resume*" - at least as it may compare to those of others. They have never led men or groups, and perhaps never even been part of a team, sports or otherwise.

We ask these men to join in our lodge activities, learn an odd way of speaking, and perhaps run some committees and projects. Along the way, they learn they have an affinity for planning and organizing, and they begin to compile a resume of small "victories", a successful lodge project, learning a key role in a degree, or even becoming an instructor for new candidates. Our new mason is coming out of his shell, and it is noticed by his brothers who nominate and elect him to the line and watch as he moves through the chairs, now with fresh experience and new confidence he's gained only through his masonic experience.

Each position became a title - "Committee Chairman", "Senior Deacon", "Senior Warden", "Worshipful Master", and even "Past Master"; all titles that reflect a man's achievements. Achievements of a curious man who came to the door maybe eight or nine years ago with no experience and no leadership or communication skills. He occasionally pauses to consider his progress and sees how he has "leveled up" from that shy, unaccomplished self that he remembers so well.

It probably comes as no surprise to anyone when our brother is recognized and appointed to a District Deputy position, except perhaps to the brother himself. He did not seek it; in fact, the idea had never occurred to him. However, there was an honor: appreciation for his time and skills, which he had donated willingly to his lodge and to masonry, as well as recognition of his achievements and a record of completing his work according to his instructions. He is about to "level up" again.

Then come the demeaning and spiteful comments on social media about "*title chasers*". He is not immune to these posts and this quasi-public ridicule. "*Title chasers*" are typically denigrated by supposed brothers who have never met them and know nothing of their masonic histories, personal growth, or ambitions. Should we infer these keyboard warriors are *not* seeking to "*level up*" because it's "*not cool*"? Perhaps their definition of "*making good men better*" is different than those whom they brand as "*title chasers*", but are they entitled to believe their definition is the *only* definition?

We see similar social media debates about pin or bling collectors and about what we wear to lodge. Those who enjoy dressing it up a bit are accused of snobbery or elite thinking, and bling collectors are merely ridiculed and dismissed. At no point in these often-heated online discussions are the individual brothers considered, in fact, as brothers who may have their objectives for their Masonic membership and their measures of improvement and progress. It strikes me as ironic that these arguments seem to come from many who appear satisfied to join a fraternity whose motto is "*Making Good Men Better,*" with personal goals of remaining exactly as they were the day they were initiated.

We tell each man that masonry can make a good man better, but that it is, in fact, up to each man to define "*better*" for himself *and what that improvement is measured against*. Why is it then okay to hold a brother up to public ridicule for walking a path that is different than others and for valuing rewards and recognition in a way that is different than their own? It all feels a bit unseemly to me.

When a man who has never been in a position to lead or to succeed in some fashion suddenly finds himself in a position to be recognized and rewarded for his efforts, perhaps that recognition holds much different value and meaning to him that other brothers who are searching for other things, other achievements, or other recognition along the path of their particular masonic journeys.

In my view of this matter and in light of my "*evolved pondering*", I have to wonder if perhaps at least some of these brothers who are these so-called title chasers are, in fact, really just "*leveling up*".

"ON TIME" & "MASONRY IN A CHANGING CULTURE – A FOLLOW-UP"

May 14, 2024

BACKSTAGE PASS: This post is actually two posts in one; one that discusses the concept of time, and a second that provides a brief update to a lengthy article I wrote about masonry in our changing culture[3]. As I have grown older, I have become increasingly aware of the passage of time and what it truly means. This post addresses that idea briefly, and then it proceeds to the update on my paper regarding our craft's survival in a changing culture. As with all other posts, this has been edited for readability, grammar, and punctuation.

**

My brethren, it has been many weeks since I last checked in here on my blog, so I wanted to share a quick thought and provide some brief updates on the things that have been keeping me busy.

I've spent much of my recent time focused - *coincidentally* – on time. I've written about time in previous papers and blog posts, and I've invested a lot of effort on the subject throughout my "*Noah's Quest*" book series. After (roughly) three intense years studying, investing, sharing, and writing about time, there is one lesson I want to share again because it

---

[3] *"Masonry in a Changing Culture"*, Published August 15, 2022 online at this link: https://www.amasonsjourney.com/_files/ and later in 2022 in *"Guard Well Our Craft"* by Perfect Ashlar Publishing (available on Amazon)

seems to be the most concise "summation" of the topic. That lesson is this:

"Time is the most precious and most valuable commodity we have. Money comes and goes over the course of a man's years, but once he spends time, it is gone forever and therefore should be invested wisely."

It's really that simple. Once we spend (invest) some amount of time, that's it, it's gone, and there is nothing we can do to recover it and re-use it. You get one shot at every minute you spend doing whatever it is you choose, so the question you might ask yourself is *"what is the value of this time and will my investment return that value to me in some form"*? One of our first lessons as new Masons regards the twenty-four-inch gage, and it is worth revisiting.

When I ask *"...will my investment return that value to me in some form"*, I'm not asking if you will be paid for that time (although salary in exchange for time is likely a wise and useful investment), I'm asking whether your investment will return some form of satisfaction, joy, or maybe personal growth or peace?

I will admit that I spend some amount of time on social media each day and yes, I am troubled by this fact in various ways. First, the time I spend mindlessly scrolling is never coming back to me, and I admit that sometimes the only value I receive comes in the form of brief periods of pure escapism. On the other hand, I manage various groups - masonic and non-masonic - and I share information that could be important to others. There *is* value and some satisfaction in that.

There is a seedier side to social media, and its inherently strong allure for many, which relates to my discussion of time: the issue of the *"keyboard warrior"*. I'm sure we've all noticed that many social media soldiers thrive in the cover and concealment of the keyboard and engage in provocative and, in some cases, aggressive behavior they would almost certainly avoid in face-to-face engagements with others. We can speculate endlessly on what motivates them and what it is they get from jumping from one confrontation to another, but that is not my point here today.

My point and my anchor to the topic of our time is very specific. I spend some amount of my "mindless scrolling" time browsing the various social media groups and pages, and I've noticed an increase in provocative posts and remarks that seem intended to draw brothers into keyboard confrontations; some are abrupt and challenging, but others are openly confrontational and border on insulting. I will come across such posts, read the discussion, and comments to see if any helpful or informative exchanges follow, but in many cases, the answer is no. I've seen some threads that run as long as 100 or more comments and typically result in my disappointment and even anger. This is my point.

For a thread to garner 100 or more comments means that two or more brothers invested quite a bit of their time in writing, reading, and responding to provocative and unproductive discussions that may have been started for the sheer thrill of provoking others. I know provocateurs gain some amount of personal satisfaction in luring others into keyboard ambushes, and there is nothing I can do that will influence them to stop; instead, I would ask everyone who spends their most precious commodity responding and arguing with faceless demagogues, *why do you remain engaged with those who do not value your time*? My brothers, the time you spend *"feeding the beast"* of social media arguments is gone; it's never coming back. I know how it starts because I feel it too - the thought that I have the answer or a perspective that will help the discussion in some way; but in many cases, when we offer our reasonable response, we are met with shifting arguments and moving goalposts. Once we see the battle lines forming, it is time to do our valuation - is it worth any more of my valuable time to continue this engagement?

I recommend a test of some sort - imagine something you could do instead of jumping into the fray, something that would at least return to you a small amount of personal peace or joy. Personally, when I stumble across a brewing battle, I now think to myself "you know, a root beer float would be nice right about now" and I withdraw my investment from the keyboard and reinvest it in some A&W and Blue Bell (this is not a paid ad, and I received no compensation for the references). Think about your time, my brethren. It is yours and it is valuable! You get to choose how you spend it, and once you do, it is gone - invest it wisely! I may address the topic of masons engaging in provocative and insulting arguments with brothers in a later post or paper - or I may not (it's a time issue).

This brings me to my second topic today – freemasonry in our ever-changing culture. I published a paper on August 15, 2022, called *"Freemasonry in a Changing Culture*[4]*"* about how the craft is impacted by

---

[4] And later published in my book *"Guard Well Our Craft"* in 2022 by Perfect Ashlar Publishing. It is available on Amazon.

several dramatic changes rippling throughout society, and I provided discussion on such things as the family, education, and the matters of "joining" and "finishing." One of my key takeaways from the paper was the belief that we need to focus on the elements and problems within the craft that we can address directly, rather than beating ourselves up and trying to fix things that are actually external problems emanating from the chaos of our changing society. I am pleased to announce that I plan to revisit and potentially revise my original paper and conclusions. I see positive changes—or at least indications of positive changes — in various corners of the culture, and I think it warrants a re-examination.

There appears to be a youth bracket (roughly mid-teens through mid-twenties) that craves a spiritual meaning or spiritual underpinning for their lives, and that bracket is apparently growing. I've seen enough anecdotal evidence to convince me that it is worth the investment of my time (there's that topic again) to update my original paper or to see at least if the data supports this notion of positive changes unfolding in society. So, I plan to work on that research as soon as my current writing project is finished and off to the publisher.

CATECHISMS AND FLOORWORK

March 28, 2022

BACKSTAGE PASS: This article came about after several weeks and many discussions about "improving" or "modernizing" masonry to accommodate the man of today who, presumably, doesn't have the time or desire to adhere to our various masonic traditions. I'm of that old school where I was taught that if we are to pass our craft to future generations, it should be the same craft that was handed to us by our predecessors. This article follows my thinking on this topic and, like the others, has been edited for readability, grammar, and punctuation.

✶✶

It has been a few weeks since I last reminded everyone that I am of the "*old think*" generation and I tend to cling, or at least it *seems* that I tend to adhere to our traditions and "*the way we've always done it*". While it's never been entirely accurate, and while I can be convinced to do things in new, creative, and effective ways, I do believe some Masonic traditions are the way they are for concrete reasons, reasons that go to the very heart of Masonry itself.

Two of the most common suggestions I hear from very well-intentioned brothers who want to update or modernize masonry are, first, to provide one-day classes for the degrees and second, to either de-emphasize or eliminate the catechisms (memory work). Most of those who suggest these ideas also emphasize the importance of upholding obligations, and every candidate should be required to learn and recite their obligations. Still, the catechisms they teach us are outdated and have little to no value in today's society, which is being overwhelmed by demands on our collective time. The theory is that a candidate's time is better spent quickly finishing his degrees (perhaps through a one-day class) so he can start studying masonry at his own pace, according to his own lifestyle and available time.

I beg to differ. I not only believe that the full-form, individual degrees and catechisms are critical to unlocking the mysteries of masonry and that every candidate must, in all cases, receive each degree in due and ancient form, but I also believe they must also learn and recite the associated catechisms. I'm sure this comes as no surprise to anyone who has read any of my previous writings, but please allow me to make my case.

QUESTION: Is there a need or a role in our fraternity going forward for full-form, individual degrees and their related catechisms in today's masonry? Or have they become obsolete in their current form and in need of either shortening, combining, or dropping them completely? Can we make the degree process much shorter and much more efficient by designing new or modified methods to teach new masons?

ANSWER: The degrees are the allegory used to portray and share the craft and symbolism which is the language of masonry. The full-form, individual degrees and the related catechisms are the primary tools to train the new mason's brain to think in terms of allegory and symbols and break the mason's dependence on writing and reading the written word. Through individual degrees and catechisms, the new mason learns to interpret masonic allegory and identify and understand masonic symbols - both of which are necessary for all masons to learn and internalize.

DISCUSSION: Masonry likely emerged and evolved during a historical period before the written word, and then undoubtedly continued expanding through the times when only the rich and well-connected were allowed to attend school and were taught to read. Many believe we emerged from the ancient mystery schools in Egypt, which were generally structured in a form similar to the very initiatic process we practice today.

The initiatic process employed by many ancient trades and guilds generally consisted of ceremonies where a candidate was imbued with necessary knowledge according to defined increments (degrees), each built on pre-existing knowledge or preceding lessons. The goal was to bring each new member of the particular craft to a common point where they were considered to have attained the minimum level of knowledge necessary to understand their craft and interact as equals among their fellow craft members.

The floor work of the degrees teaches us the allegorical lessons and symbols of masonry, while the catechisms teach us how to see, recognize, and understand those allegories and symbols, and finally, they teach us how to communicate that knowledge using like-signs and symbols. In short, we learn masonry and its principles through the degrees and catechisms in the same form our long-passed brothers shared masonry and their collective knowledge - using only their instructive tongues to communicate the lessons to receptive ears.

Masonry was never intended to be taught through written language or text books - tools which in all likelihood did not exist at the birth of the craft. It has been passed down through all ages from one generation to the next via allegory and symbols. It is critical for masons to personally participate in the floor work to see, live, and experience the allegory, and then to learn the catechisms which we use as tools to train the mind to translate our allegories into masonic symbols, making it possible for us to understand and teach fundamental masonic principles in their true and original form.

Once properly instructed in the degrees and catechisms, the candidate's mind has been opened to think, conceive, and portray lessons allegorically, and to see, read, and understand the symbols of masonry as taught through the experiences of the degrees. But this education or training of the mind cannot happen if either the degrees or the catechisms are skipped or eliminated from the candidate's initiatic experience. If a candidate does not walk the floor during a degree, how is he then to understand the allegory such walking (circumambulation) represents? If he does not learn the symbols attached to his own actions and movements through the instruction and recitation of catechisms, how then is he to know the heart and soul of masonry in its original, symbolic form? If candidates do not see or feel this cognitive value from their investment of their time and work, then perhaps that is what is actually broken, and perhaps it is *that* which we need to fix!

Can masonry be modernized? Perhaps. However, in an era when our brothers are increasingly seeking to learn more about our Masonic history and principles, we must continue to provide the essence and core of Masonry itself in its original form, as intended by our ancestors and subsequently presented to all Masons who have traveled Masonic and mysterious paths before us. We must teach new masons how to think allegorically and identify, relate to, and apply Masonic symbols as they build their Masonic edifice. *Do we strive to become and then live as*

Masons, continuing our craft and upholding our ancestors' impressive traditions? Or do we seek to become a group of men who simply study and talk about how Masons historically shared their craft?

Masonry and all of its beauty is contained in its full form within our allegories and symbols, and it is up to *us* to seek them and teach new masons how to share them in historically due form if we are to propagate our craft and its beautiful principles into the future!

Travel on my worthy brothers!

BroBill

IN AND ABOUT THE LODGE

SHOULD I BELONG TO TWO LODGES?

April 24, 2022

BACKSTAGE PASS: Just some passing thoughts on the age-old question of multiple memberships in multiple lodges and multiple organizations. Not too deep and not very controversial, just some stream of consciousness on this enduring dilemma. I have edited it somewhat for readability and grammar.

**

For many brothers, the first question that occurs to them upon being raised is "York Rite or Scottish Rite"? Or perhaps they ask if it's "time to Shrine"? Let me pose another, perhaps more valuable question. "Two lodges or *not* two lodges"? Simply put, should we belong to two blue lodges?

I would answer enthusiastically, "Yes, by all means, if you can afford to join a second lodge, do it"!

Anyone who has browsed my bio on my website will see that I am a member of three subordinate lodges, and I am actually only active in two of them[5]. Based on my own experience, I would suggest that belonging to and being active in two lodges is a good thing and a good idea.

---

[5] As of the time I compiled this book, I have become active again in my third lodge and am now active in all three of my lodges.

The first and most important reason (in my personal estimation) for joining a second lodge is that you immediately extend your masonic network and expand your growing circle of brothers and friends. Every brother you meet and come to know becomes another priceless source of experience, ideas, and knowledge.

Next, the act of finding a second lodge takes you on the road as you travel to and visit lodges, meet new brothers, and learn the courtesies and protocols of being a visitor in a lodge. You might spend several weeks or several months searching for that second lodge, but that's okay. Take your time, find that lodge that's a good fit for you and maybe offers things your mother lodge does not. This could take several visits to several lodges, but that's the fun of traveling! You may find yourself participating in degrees or maybe just attending social events. Still, in any or all of these situations, you meet a lot of brothers, and you learn more and more about masonry and life in different lodges.

THE SEAT IN THE EAST - VIRTUES OF A MASTER

March 31, 2023

BACKSTAGE PASS: This article is closely tied to "Working Tools of a Worshipful Master" and, in fact, actually led to it. Sometimes an idea will bound around in my mind for a while before it finally pops out through the keyboard. I have cleaned it up a bit with some edits for readability and grammar.

⁂

The Worshipful Master of my lodge handed me a book ("*Worshipful Master's Guidebook; Or the Book of Joe*" by Bro. James F. Hatcher III, PM). As he passed it to me, he opened it and showed me that the first section contained the author's thoughts and content, while the rest of the book was filled only with blank lines. On these lines, the Master informed me, current and past masters can write their thoughts and ideas for their successors to "*The Seat in the East,*" and he then asked me to provide some input to this small, paper-bound treasure chest of ideas.

I knew what I wanted to say, but I knew I needed to play around with my words first on the computer to make sure I got it right; as it started coming together in a draft document, I realized it would also serve as a good blog post. So here we go, a longer version of my input to our lodge's "master's diary" (as it were) for you to ponder.

My brother, congratulations on your election to "*The Seat in the East*", the dawn and place of light for our lodge as well as all lodges formed in the name and spirit of our great fraternity. You have been elected by brothers not because it's your turn, but because they are ready and willing to invest their hopes for the future of the lodge in you and in your ability to lead the brethren and care for our common unity that binds us in brotherhood.

Worshipful Sir, you have *three duties and obligations* while you occupy The Seat in the East. First, you *must* maintain harmony in and about the lodge; second, you must communicate your vision for your year and the lodge; and third, you must maintain the unity of the lodges over which you now (or soon will) preside. Why do I say "*lodges*"? Ah, there is clarification coming... please bear with me as this was not an accident.

My brother, your primary and most important duty to the brethren is to maintain **harmony** in and about the lodge. Without harmony, the door is open to discord that will disrupt the lodge, the brotherly love among the members, and the order necessary to the life of your lodges. While you might help with the work of your committees and provide leadership on projects and your objectives, your officers and the brethren are charged to execute your vision and operate in their necessary stations and places to keep the lodge running. They are best able to do their several duties in an atmosphere where peace and harmony prevail. This is your charge, this is the challenge of your imminent legacy!

Next, my brother, you must communicate your **vision** for your year and the lodge to the brethren because without this knowledge, the brethren cannot unify behind a common goal and a common objective. Once the unity of purpose is lost, or worse if it is never established, forward progress then comes to a halt, and the door is open for discord and chaos. **Unity** of effort is a powerful and binding force for good when shared among brethren with a desire to serve, becoming a powerful tool binding the brethren into a lodge and defining their common destination - use it!

Finally, my brother, Worshipful Sir, you must ensure your lodges are unified for the common good of the brethren. I used the word "lodges" again and again; it is no accident. Our craft is of a unique legacy of operative and speculative lodges. In a manner, we have continued these traditions, and we exist today in the duality of both of these historical lodges – *the operative and speculative.*

The **operative lodge** over which you will preside consists of the building, the lodge room, and the brethren laboring with and amongst each other to operate the West Gate and maintain our home and its very heart. It is the operative lodge that commands much of our attention as officers and leaders of the lodge; it is most prominent among our senses.

The **speculative lodge**, on the other hand, is often neglected, under-nurtured, and typically receives what one might call "short shrift" when it comes to attention and care. Worshipful Master, your *speculative lodge is that spirit that unites the brothers into one purpose* - it is not the objective, it is the *force* that binds the many members and brothers into a lodge for the purpose of sharing and perpetuating masonry from one generation to the next. It is the speculative lodge that gives a brother the feeling of being home among brothers and being a necessary part of the greater good of any given Masonic Lodge.

How do you pay due and necessary attention to a speculative lodge? My brother, you must communicate with all of your brothers and members! Not just the brothers that arrive and cross through the door of your operative lodge to conduct business, no, you must reach out to those brothers who are estranged for whatever reason from your lodge - brothers that have moved out of state, brothers who live too far to drive to lodge, brothers who are now unable to drive to lodge, and even those brothers who have merely drifted away, possibly because they feel unnecessary and forgotten.

As Worshipful Master, _you_ must reunite these brothers with their lodge and recreate that spiritual link, the tie that binds our distant, individual brothers into our speculative lodge of brothers, ready to serve (as limitations allow) and craving the brotherhood they miss. You will find that when these neglected and forgotten brothers are reunited with their brothers, _even if just spiritually_, they crave the contact and the news of the lodge and look for ways to return to the fold, even if geographically separated.

I implore you, Worshipful Sir, unite our speculative lodge with the operative lodge, revive the spirit that binds our brothers into "_our_" lodge, working together in our own several and various ways to keep hope and keep the brotherhood alive and well. You will be amazed at the grace and brotherly love that is waiting "_on the bench_" to be brought back onto the field and into the fold to feel again like an important part of the fraternal whole!

These three points - maintaining harmony, providing vision, and uniting the speculative lodge - constitute, in my opinion, the three principal virtues of a Worshipful Master - *harmony, vision, and unity.* Tap into them and draw the strength and wisdom necessary to guide the lodge through the ensuing year, through your year.

These, Worshipful Sir, are my thoughts and my best recommendations to you. Congratulations again, and good luck to you in your year in *"The Seat in the East"*!

WHO COULD LOVE THE CEREMONIAL "READING OF THE MINUTES"?

November 24, 2023

BACKSTAGE PASS: I have always been fascinated and disappointed by the contempt many brothers seem to hold for hearing the ceremonial "reading of the minutes" at our business meetings; so much so, I've written several articles that address this issue or at least mention it in passing. Here is a November 2023 post that tackles this puzzling issue head-on. I've edited slightly for readability and grammar.

**

Who could love listening to the ceremonial "*Reading of Minutes Not Already Read and Approved*"? Me! I love listening to the minutes, and I'll be happy to explain why!

How do we know so much about when our founding masonic fathers were initiated, passed, and raised? How do we know so much about their "home" lodges? How do we know so much about the various ceremonies, processions, and feasts their lodges held in those days so long ago? Well, obviously there was some amount of public press reporting on these affairs, but there were also various times where academics, historians, and curious masons gained valuable insight from their particular formal lodge histories which themselves take much – *if not most* – of their factual information from summaries of their accumulated *meeting minutes*. This is why we take minutes at our meetings and publish formal lodge histories - to provide insight and factual information regarding the activities of our lodges and our members in a form that is authoritative, accurate, and available for historical research.

When we take upon ourselves this duty of "*reading the minutes of not already read and approved*", we are laboring together with equal interest in the current-day success of the lodge, and we are reviewing the actions and statements made at previous meetings to ensure the historical record is correct. The Law Book of our Grand Jurisdiction requires the Worshipful Master to decide upon the correctness of the minutes and to order the correction of any error at the very first Stated Meeting after discovery. This therefore is a very specific obligation of the presiding Worshipful Master - *ensuring the historical record of the lodge is complete and correct*. As members, it is – *or should be* – our obligation to participate and assist the Worshipful Master by hearing those minutes read in front of all assembled brethren and advising him when we hear errors or if we identify important omissions. We labor *together* to ensure the history of our lodge is complete and accurate - not perhaps for our own use tomorrow, but for the eventual use by lodge brothers, masonic historians, and masonic researchers in the future.

For those who might believe that the meeting minutes of the lodge serve no immediate purpose or use, I would invite you to volunteer to participate in your next annual lodge audit where you might find yourself chasing an expenditure or an uncategorized sum of money through the minutes to determine its origin and purpose! I would be willing to bet that those brothers who have served (*and who may frequently serve*) on their lodge Audit Committee listen to the minutes from a far different perspective than brothers who have not!

In 2020, I wrote an article titled *"If Your Masonry is Based on Stated Meetings, Perhaps You're Doing It Wrong!"*[6] and I addressed this same question of reading the minutes at that time as well. Lodges have rituals to do, ritual practices to conduct, social events, educational programs, and various other activities that bring our members together at the lodge. A Stated Meeting is merely one opportunity every month to stop, review our finances and historical records, read and ballot on petitions, and tend to the business and future of the lodge. It can be made to be (or to seem) like some arduous and demanding task, or it might instead be seen as a social experience where we gather with our brothers and meet - without the pressure of memorizing and practicing ritual or instructing candidates - for the sole purpose of addressing the *operative* needs of the lodge itself.

In my mind (yes, my personal opinion, this is an *"opinion piece"* after all) the way a Stated Meeting is viewed by the members is shaped by the senior members and mentors of the lodge. If they constantly talk about them as wasteful, horrendous, and torturous gatherings that serve no value, then that is how our *new members* will come to view them and then - believe it or not - those new members will stop coming - *a particular danger for lodges that may only hold one gathering per month.*

---

[6] This article can still be found on my website at www.amasonsjourney.com/library

A Stated Meeting is what *WE* make it, and making sure that our historical record is accurate is just one of our various obligations that we attach! We may or may not write our lodge history this year or next, but perhaps some brother in the future will take the time and initiative to produce the official record of our lodge, and it is up to us to ensure that record is complete! Is ten minutes out of one night each month really too much time to commit to verifying our historical record? In fact, it is specifically because it will most likely be at some *distant* time that a brother tackles our lodge history that we owe him the courtesy *today* of capturing the activities and events of our day in such a way that they are easily understood long after those who were present and who participated are gone.

MENTORING IN MASONRY

June 15, 2021

BACKSTAGE PASS: Mentoring has always struck me as the most important – *and most underused* – tool in our craftsman tool kit. This post is one of my earliest blog posts on the subject of mentoring, but I had actually been writing on this subject for several years by this point. It felt like the blog would give me yet another avenue where I could sound the alarm about the state of mentorship within our fraternity, so here again is that early post, slightly edited for readability and grammar.

**

I have just published my latest paper, "*Living the Journey: Mentoring in Masonry.*"[7]. I published it on my website, and it is available to read online under "*Papers*" or download from my "*Library*". It is a lengthy (lengthier

---

[7] This article is available on my website at: www.amasonsjourney.com/library

than intended) examination of the criticality of mentoring, who our mentors are, the type of training they need, and how a Worshipful Master can make mentoring an effective force in his lodge.

The topic of mentoring is a very personal topic for me. While I didn't understand it at the time, my first brush with masonic mentoring was in 1997 when I had to learn my degree proficiency work. My instructor was someone I had known for many years, and I already looked upon him as my mentor. However, as I came to understand how the proficiency catechisms would work, I tried several times to tell him that I needed to hear full sentences, and then I needed to recite them back. I asked him pointedly Please don't stop me in the middle of a sentence, let me finish, and then tell me what the full sentence should be. We continued on, and he continued stopping me at every incorrect word to make me recite that word. Each session became almost unbearable, and my mind was more focused on how much more he was going to make me try to learn rather than what it was I was actually learning or what it meant.

I made a point of explaining that I cannot learn with that style of instruction. If I don't hear the words in the correct context, I quickly get confused and forget where I am in the text and what it is that the words and sentences mean. I took the full year to complete my EA proficiency, and I hated every minute of it. I came to believe that there was some rule that said instructors must stop candidates and correct them at every instance of an incorrect word. As I proceeded through my Fellowcraft and Master Mason's proficiency work, I had the same instructor, so there was no change in the style he used for instructing.

I was initiated in 1997 and wasn't raised until 1999, and came to detest the proficiency work. By the time I turned in my Master Mason's proficiency, I couldn't have told you what any of it meant, but I could tell you the order of the words. I was glad it was over, and I hoped never to have to go through anything like that again.

Unfortunately, this seems to be the dominant instruction style for teaching not only catechisms, but lodge officers' scripts and degree roles. I experience the same problem almost every time I need to learn new work. It seems that no matter how many times I try to explain that I need to learn in full sentences, 99% of everyone who instructs me will use the same confusing style - teach two or three words at a time and stop me at every incorrect word. To this day, I do not voluntarily seek new roles to learn unless they are necessary for an office or in cases where I have to fill in on a degree team. The instruction style frustrates me, confuses me, and actively prevents me from learning the meaning and context of the work. Those watching me do memory work through either a degree or an officer role may be able to detect where a previous instructor "broke up" sentences to teach me in groups of words instead of full sentences.

I tell you this as a personal example of how and where we may be falling short in our instruction and mentoring. We don't always serve our candidates well in our sharing of knowledge and information because we don't always take the time to find out important things about them - simple things like "*how do you learn*"? And we don't seem to invest our own time and effort into providing their instruction in the style *they need to enable them to learn* effectively and perhaps even easily.

We tend to brush off a candidate's preferred/needed learning style by telling them, "This is difficult work because of the phrasing, which is old and very different from the grammar we use today," and then proceed to try to teach them using a style that frustrates and, sometimes, confuses them. How many Entered Apprentices do you think we may have lost along the way simply due to the fact that they couldn't learn the work because of the style in which the instruction was provided?

Having lived with this personal experience and frustration for 21 years, it seems appropriate to use it now as an example to highlight our need in the fraternity to address how we teach and how we mentor. Our mentors and instructors are our front line, *"first responders"* for our candidates, not only providing them instruction and educational material, but also learning about them and how we might help them absorb the firehose of information we need to provide.

To mentors and instructors, I beg you to take some time with your candidate before you even start teaching them their work, and ask them *how they learn.* They may not be sure, so you can try various versions and see how they respond. Do they need to hear two or three words at a time? Do they need to hear full sentences? Do they need to hear a sentence in plain English first, followed by the same sentence in the form and style of our catechisms? Maybe they need to learn the questions and answers so the material flows and makes contextual sense.

If our instructors spend some time at the very beginning, it may prove to be a valuable investment that helps our candidates, degree teams, and officers absorb and apply the work that is necessary if we are to continue and maintain our unique traditions and protocols into the future.

We lose a lot of brothers between the time they are initiated and the time they should be raised. We often look (correctly) at whether we have missed something in our investigation, or if we spent enough time with them before allowing them to petition. Yes, those are important aspects in advancing new masons, but let's not overlook how we mentor, how we instruct, and how our candidates are receiving and learning their material.

We owe our candidates and all future masons an experience - a unique experience that is distinct from all other social and professional organizations they have to choose from when they ponder knocking on our door. It is up to us to not only know what that experience should be, but also to be experts in how we provide it and how we instruct and explain it. I think if we can improve our mentoring and instruction techniques, we will also solve at least a portion of our retention problem.

Brethren, please go to my website at www.amasonsjourney.com and find my paper, "*Living the Journey: Mentoring in Masonry*" under "*Papers*", or go to the "*Library*" page and download it.

My brethren, I remain sincerely and fraternally yours!

Bro. Bill Boyd, Past Master,

Valley-Hi Lodge No. 1407

MENTORING ON THE FLY

December 12, 2023

BACKSTAGE PASS: Mentoring has always been a sticky subject for me. We hammer home the need to mentor, but we give no instruction, education, or – *ironically enough* – mentorship on mentoring! I have written other articles on mentoring, and I even incorporated an entire section of my "*Lodge Education Manual*" on why and how to mentor, but today it remains an art that doesn't even begin to approach a science, at least within our craft. This post is but one of my efforts to instill the idea of mentoring among our lodge leaders and provide some specific examples. The article has been edited for readability, grammar, and punctuation.

**

Let's call this post a "*Mentor's Minute*" - a quick tip for strengthening our lodge experience. As a general rule, people hate doing things with no explanation as to why they are doing it or what the value of the job or the particular task is. This is especially true of our Entered Apprentices and Fellowcrafts, and perhaps even a few of our Master Masons who are still relatively new to the craft and to the lodge experience.

Those same brothers may find they are getting bored in meetings while the Worshipful Master and Brethren are discussing business they do not understand, and, as I think we have seen, when they get bored in meetings, they tend to stop attending. The solution? Turn every meeting into a learning experience and "*mentor on the fly*" or explain as you go.

During the course of your stated meeting, especially if you are in the East, you should explain to new masons what you're talking about, how it fits into their budding masonic experience, and why it's important. New masons are already overwhelmed with their memory work and their new meetings and commitments, so the more we can help them make sense of it all and show them how it all fits together, the higher the likelihood they will join in and participate.

We inundate our new masons with all types of masonic jargon and lingo, so let's explain it to them so they feel they are part of the discussion.

Who or what is this D.D.G.M. everyone seems so concerned about? Why can't I attend when our lodge receives them? The Worshipful Master can easily explain this to new masons as he holds the discussion about preparations for an upcoming D.D.G.M. visit.

What is the audit, and why do we do it? The Worshipful Master should be able to explain this in about two sentences.

Why do we do "Sickness and Distress," and why do we drape the charter? What are the rules for draping the charter? A brief sentence or two should clarify all of this and make the new brothers comfortable enough to join in and share any concerns, illnesses, or distress they may have.

There are many things we discuss, move, and vote on in a Stated Meeting, and in many cases, we've slipped into an unending stream of casual slang or jargon, and we often leave our new brothers out or leave them behind as we rocket our way through our business.

Explain your business to those who will have to conduct it in the future! Make the new brothers part of the discussions, and when they can't participate, explain why. Importantly, explain why the matters you are discussing at today's meetings might affect them in the future - *show them through active mentoring how all of the pieces and parts fit together* - this is how the future line officers learn the expectations and responsibilities of the offices and what it takes to run the lodge. This is how we train our leaders! Every brother abandoned to the blizzard of jargon is a candidate to be the next brother who abandons your meetings and your lodge!

Mentor on the fly! Engage your EAs and FCs!

S&F

-BroBill

BASIC MILITARY TRAINING – OR BASIC MASONIC TRAINING?

February 28, 2025

BACKSTAGE PASS: This was a "fun" piece that let me discuss the state of masonic education in our fraternity, a topic that always lurks in the back of my mind and occasionally slips out into public in various forms and venues. This article is intended to stimulate thought and discussion about how we deliver education and how effective we are at that effort. I have edited it for readability and grammar as needed.

⁎⁎

I'm sure you've heard of *"Basic Military Training,"* which is the term used for the U.S. Air Force version of military boot camp, but have you ever heard of *"Basic Masonic Training"*? I would wager a guess that you have not. I'm sure it never occurred to you to compare basic military training to early masonic education, but here we are, and I am about to take you somewhere you've never been – *if you're willing to follow me!*

What is basic military training? It is the initiation of a recruited civilian into a new profession and a new way of life. What is the craft lodge? It is where we initiate the curious candidate into a new way of life and prepare them for their eventual rebirth as a new person. Both basic military training and the craft lodge are the first step in an initiatic process intended to break a man away from his past, help him shed his former self, and prepare him for an entirely new purpose in his life.

Basic training separates a man from his family for a period of time, breaking the dependence on family and allowing the recruit to learn how to tap into and depend on their inner strength to accomplish tasks and objectives. In our craft lodges, we separate the candidate from the outside world through the secrecy of our tiled meetings, providing a secluded environment where they can absorb the necessary lessons and ultimately draw upon their inner strength and desire to move forward in life. In our lodges, we also isolate the candidate from external influences with our veil of secrecy, which prevents them from being drawn to the irrelevant or distracting noise of society for direction. Just as the military *physically* separates and isolates its recruits, masonry *spiritually* separates and isolates our candidates.

Basic military training involves ritualistic training, including formations, marching, customs and courtesies (such as saluting), and drill. The craft lodge provides its early lessons through ritualistic degrees that include circumambulation, instruction, and commands provided from The East.

Basic military training offers classroom instruction on service history, traditions, and law, and our craft lodges provide instruction on the catechisms (memory work), history, traditions, and law.

Basic military training requires recruits to prove their fitness through written exams and physical tests, and our craft lodge requires new masons to prove their readiness through oral and written examinations (the Additional Lodge Light program in Texas).

Basic military training culminates in a final graduation ceremony, complete with formal military drill, replete with pomp and circumstance, and then the new service member is launched into the military world as a new member of an elite group. In our craft lodges, we (might) congratulate our new mason and present him a certificate before we bid him to take his rightful seat on the sideline among his brothers.

At the end of the two initiations, we find similar results; in one we see a new, confident service member, steeped in the rules and traditions of his service on his way to his first duty station where his training will continue and, with the help of his brothers in arms, he will grow and advance according to the level of effort he invests in his career and future. The mason will assume his seat on the sideline, and he, too, will grow and advance in masonry and his life according to the level of effort he invests in his future.

My goal with this impromptu exercise was to demonstrate how basic military training and fundamental Masonic training share objectives and similarities in purpose and function. Now that I have laid out my conceptual comparison, let's do a little troubleshooting to see if it holds up under scrutiny.

In many of our lodges, a new mason memorizes some scripts and recites them to the satisfaction of his brother lodge members and then is pronounced *"knowledgeable"* in the craft for that degree; *are they really?* When a servicemember completes his written and physical tests, you can be sure he has met a clearly defined and measured standard and attained a well-defined level of knowledge regarding his new profession. Is there any standard level of knowledge – *beyond the ability to memorize a script* – that actually confirms that a new mason is qualified or proficient in the craft?

The craft lodges are charged with conferring the *first* three degrees in masonry. Their highest priority and principal function is to prepare men for their travels as masons and prepare them for the additional degrees that are available and waiting in the other orders. Are we preparing our new masons with the knowledge and experience necessary to function in the world of masonry and – *more importantly* – make personal decisions on the quality, direction, and destinations of their masonic journeys?

Perhaps it is time to consider some type of ordered, progressive education program that sets objectives and defines progressive tasks (meaning sequenced in a progressive order) and performance challenges to achieve them. We might design a one- or two-year program that is organized according to key components of our craft, such as symbolism, ritual, and history; notice I left out lodge operation, and I did that intentionally because most jurisdictions already have some form of lodge leadership training programs. In my mind, this concept would focus on the more sublime and esoteric aspects of our craft – *the mysteries.*

I would *not* design this educational regimen as a "pass-fail" course of instruction, rather as a "progress check" or a "completed or non-completed" checklist, and it might be tracked in the brother's record, whether that might be Grandview or some other variation found in other jurisdictions.

This idea is merely conceptual and certainly not *"ready for prime time"*; my objective here is to plant a seed, to perhaps move some of our brothers to take some action or actions to commit our lodges and the craft to our newest generations of brothers with the same zeal our armed forces commit to their new recruits – take them by the arm and teach them! Provide our new brothers with the single most critical working tool of all: knowledge. This is the essential tool necessary for us to preserve the craft and for new masons to design and follow their masonic journey.

I suppose this is a good opportunity for a shameless plug for my "Lodge Education Manual," which I wrote several years ago. It's posted on my website in a downloadable (pdf) format[8]. It is designed in blocks so you may find some duplication between chapters, but this way, a lodge can use the manual to create an educational program based on its unique lodge needs. I finished work on the most recent edition in 2021 and proudly posted it as the "Official Bootleg Copy," which is free for any lodge to use if they like. The centerpiece of the manual is the "phase" system, where I identify specific phases in a mason's journey and match knowledge, skills, reading lists, and some sources to each phase. My warning would be this: This manual is based on the Grand Lodge of Texas work and law book, and there have been a few minor changes since 2021. However, on the whole, you should be able to develop some ideas for your lodge using this version. If you are interested in the manual, you can download the document at no cost.

---

[8] "Lodge Education Manual – Official Bootleg Copy" is posted on www.amasonsjourney.com/library"

The military is obligated to provide their recruits with the knowledge and training necessary to improve the servicemember's chance of surviving in battle and to provide them with the skill needed to contribute to military success on the battlefield. In masonry, a craft handed down from one generation to the next by way of the knowledgeable tongue to the attentive ear, we *are obligated* to provide our newest masons with the knowledge and education necessary to pass our masonic story to following generations accurately; are we, or are we *not* our brothers' keepers? It seems to me that we are entrusted with the mysteries of our craft and the legacies of our brothers who have gone before us, and it is up to us to pass them on into the future by teaching them to each and every new mason in each and every new generation.

My brothers, next time you are sitting around your lodge or dining room, passing the time, why not put your heads together and create an educational experience for new masons in your lodge? A lodge well-founded on solid knowledge of our mysteries and the history of the craft is also a lodge that is well-positioned for a long and healthy future!

I want to thank you for your time and your consideration; may brotherly love prevail, and every moral and social virtue cement us!

~BroBill

A Mason's Journey

A LETTER TO MY BROTHER

May 28,2025

BACKSTAGE PASS: The trend is not our friend. I've been watching numbers and other data points in my lodges and my other organizations and participation is definitely down. It's odd; we are initiating new brothers, and we are gaining new members in my appendant bodies. Where is everyone? Yes, our initiation and new member petitions are lower than they were five or six years ago, but there has been an increase in membership numbers year over year. Yet the sidelines at meetings are empty, and turnout at our social and fundraising events is at the lowest levels ever. The situation has prompted me to take to the keyboard and try to sift through the thoughts that are bouncing around in my mind.

**

To my close and fraternal brother, how are you? It has been a very long time since we have enjoyed your company across the dinner table or in the lodge. I hope all is well, I know you are very busy with your work and all of your various professional and masonic commitments. Since it's been so long, I wanted to take a brief moment and let you know how your mother lodge is faring of late.

I'm afraid the current situation here is not very good. In fact, I would say the state of affairs in and about our lodge might accurately be described as quite grim. If you were to look just at our numbers you might say we appear quite healthy, but numbers alone can be quite deceiving. Yes, it's true, we initiate five or six new masons every year, but sadly we only raise two or three. And yes, it is also true that our membership shows well over one hundred living members, but in reality, fewer than twenty of our brothers attend lodge on a regular basis. One might be forgiven for wondering where all of our living brothers are and how many of them might be available and physically able to attend lodge but simply do not?

You might remember several years ago during your year in the East when every officer chair was full and our meetings had twenty or twenty-five brothers filling the seating along the sides; but it saddens me to tell you today that we no longer fill every officer seat at every meeting and we don't even fill them at election time. In fact, on election night we are normally only able fill as far down as the Deacons' chairs (and sometimes those just barely); it's been years since we've seated a Steward, and I can't remember when we last filled the Marshal or Master of Ceremonies chairs. On meeting nights, we do manage to fill the chairs of most of our elected and appointed officers, but we only see eight to ten brothers on the sides; it's just not the same as you probably remember.

If you were to visit today, you would find a few brothers hanging around in the dining room, passing time, shooting the breeze, and a few others perhaps working on their memory work with their instructors. But when we walk together into the lodge room, I think you might be surprised to find that there is an entire generation – *possibly two* – that is completely missing. Our Senior Warden was raised four years ago, and our Junior Warden just two years ago. We were fortunate this year to initiate, pass, and raise a new brother with years of clerical experience from his job, and he cheerfully stepped in to fill our vacant Secretary's position, and we are about to observe his one-year masonic birthday at our next Stated Meeting.

While we struggle now every year to fill out our elective line, our Past Masters that still attend are occupied fully with conferring degrees and instructing candidates. They've all been through the chairs at least two times – and one or two of *them* three times – and have no desire to return to the East; these lodge elders are hard at work trying their best to prepare our next generation of brothers. Our lodge has very few mentors to act as the models for our new masons, and who can share important lessons on how to manage and run the lodge, or how to apply masonry in one's life. It is somewhat ironic that our most active and experienced brothers also spend valuable personal time traveling to other local lodges to help their brothers confer degrees, and some have even affiliated with them in order to help *them* fill out *their* officer lines. It saddens me a little when I tell you our lodge is not unique in any regard in this need for experienced brothers and role models.

Some of our key positions, like Secretary and Treasurer, change every year or every other year and the duties are inevitably handed to a new brother who has never held an elective or appointive position; there is little, if any, continuity and therefore virtually no one who can spot problems or dangerous trends in our lodge data and records. Indeed, it is only the Past Masters and a few of our oldest active members who have read our lodge bylaws or even know the process to change them.

I am also sorry to tell you that many of our favorite lodge traditions are becoming unsustainable. We no longer draw enough volunteers from among the members to organize and run our regular programs, and they will likely become unviable very soon. There are now only a few members who still turn out to provide their time and the necessary labor and to help make our social events and fundraisers successful. There are no functioning committees, and very few of our new members seem committed to the lodge or interested in serving in a chair in line. Without a strong cadre of active members and Past Masters to lead the way and excite our new generation, I am afraid our most treasured memories and traditions will soon fall by the wayside. My brother, the lodge today is very different from it was when you last attended.

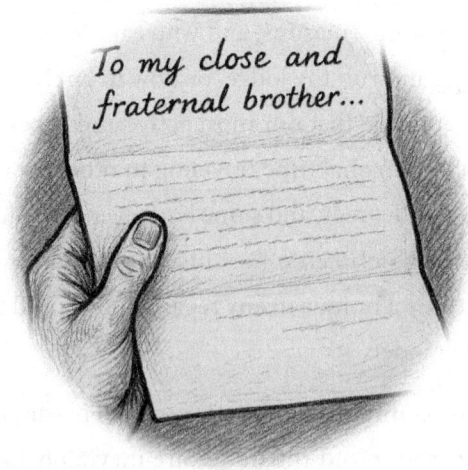

So, how are *you* doing, my friend? I hope life is good for you. I know it's hectic. I have always admired your search for additional light, your personal *"treasure hunt"* for knowledge. I know how much you enjoy your labors in the York and Scottish Rites, and I also understand that the important work of you and our many Shrine brothers is indispensable in improving the lives of children and their families. You have enjoyed a rich masonic journey with each organization adding their particular squared and polished ashlars to your personal edifice, and I trust that your quest for masonic fellowship will continue to lead you to further light.

Your journey could serve as a valuable (or even priceless) model for this next generation of brothers who are searching; they are in the very early years of their travels, and they aren't yet sure what it is that they might be seeking. It is a shame these fine men who are thirsty for knowledge and role models don't have more access to you, your experiences, and all of the new and intriguing experiences you have gained through your masonic travels. Brothers such as yourself have found and now carry so much light, light that might be shared with a new generation of masons seeking inspiration and direction in their own lives and young masonic journeys, but how will you share this priceless treasure? How will you spread that light? How can you serve as that beacon in the darkness for our brothers if all of your time and attention is consumed outside of our lodge? It is quite a dilemma indeed, and I do not claim to know the answer.

My brother, I would never presume to estimate the length of your cable tow or to judge your masonic journey because I cannot possibly know your personal struggles and concerns. We are each responsible for our own choices and, indeed, I would likewise be somewhat offended if a brother offered an uninformed judgment of my own decisions or on the purpose and quality of my personal masonic journey; instead, I would ask you simply this: Please share your zeal! Your lodge and our next generation of masons need you, and they need access to all the knowledge and life experience you've gained from your masonic journey! The load for those laboring in lodge will soon be too heavy to bear and we need help; our active and experienced brothers need a rest, and they need the "*missing generation*" to step in and step up where they can. We need role models and mentors with ideas and experiences if we are to have any hope of leading the lodge – *your lodge* – into the future with well-informed, well-instructed, and well-practiced brothers!

My brother, your mother lodge is calling, will you answer?

NOTE FROM AMJ: *The thoughts expressed in this fictional letter do NOT refer to any one particular lodge; rather, it describes a composite of many lodges that are experiencing troubling times and worrisome challenges.*

SYMBOLISM AND ALLEGORY

TRAVELING GATE-TO-GATE

January 27, 2022

BACKSTAGE PASS: This post has an interesting lineage. This post is directly tied to the origin of Noah Lewis and *"Noah's Quest: Trial at the Gate."*[9]. After that first book came out, I was stuck with Noah Lewis at the beginning of some story I had not yet defined. My obsession with masonic symbolism and my quest for hidden allegories was born in late 2021, and I have been using Noah Lewis to search for hidden messages from the GAOTU ever since. This post is part of my own internal struggle over how masonry and its beautiful lessons manifest in our lives. I have edited it somewhat for readability and grammar.

**

I've extracted and expanded on some thoughts from one of my papers (*"Living the Journey: What Comes after "Better"?*[10]), published on October 14, 2021, and posted under "Papers" and my "Library", and the result follows.

---

[9] Published originally in 2021 by Perfect Ashlar Publishing and republished in 2024 as a Second Edition. Can be purchased through Amazon.
[10] Can be found and downloaded in my web library: www.amasonsjourney.com/library

I like to say that as masons, we travel on a journey from gate to gate. We all start at the same "*west gate*", metaphorically speaking, and then travel our own, individual paths on our way to the Pearly Gate. We start on the level and follow our interests and inclinations as we move individually through our lives, making our own decisions and learning our own lessons as we go, hoping to eventually find ourselves at a common, ultimate destination —the next and final gate.

As we travel, masonry occasionally forces us to confront our mortality and ponder the immortality of our souls. It provides us with "waypoints" where we pause and ponder our present direction on our chosen path and our ultimate destination and destiny. A brother may at any moment tell us of the passing of a brother, and so we join our brethren and gather in his memory to provide his Masonic graveside rites. Yes, we are seeing our brother off as he is accepted and passes through the next gate – *The Pearly Gate* – of the Celestial Lodge above for his next journey, but we should also be reminded at the same time of our mortality in this solemn moment of reflection.

It is these moments, and moments similar to these, for friends who are not masons, when we must consider our fitness, our readiness to approach and ultimately enter that next great gate. We once waited anxiously outside the Masonic West Gate; we waited to be found worthy and to be found well-qualified to enter. And our journeys will eventually take each of us to that ultimate gate where we will wait again to be judged on our worthiness and qualification to enter.

Will we have used our time and our travels wisely? Have we taken the opportunities along our paths to qualify ourselves for the moment of our arrival at this final gate and our ultimate passage? Or have we failed to learn from our experience at the west gate? You see, that was our very first lesson in masonry, that allegorical appearance at a symbolic gate to be judged and deemed worthy or unworthy. I believe this lesson presented an allegory for our journey to and arrival at the Pearly Gate, where we pray to be judged and found worthy. This, to me, was a *significant* preparatory lesson in masonry, teaching us that our road will one day lead us to the place and moment of ultimate judgment, and providing us with the true beginning of that journey to qualify ourselves to enter that Celestial Lodge. It taught us that it was our own free will and accord that brought us to that Masonic west gate, and it will also be our own free will that determines the result of that pending final judgement at the Pearly Gate.

We craved and heard the words "...*let him be received*..." at the west gate, but have we since used our journeys simply as an adventure, or possibly as a life that is merely to be endured, or have we *lived* it as our one true path and the means, the vehicle to prepare ourselves properly to ensure the next time we find ourselves at a gate, at "*The Gate*", we hear the words "...*well done my good and faithful servant*"?

My brother, our embrace of masonry makes it easy for us to remember the purpose of our journey. When you are struggling, when you are considering a moral question of right and wrong, simply remind yourself that as a mason, you are traveling from gate to gate.

S&F

Bro. Bill

GATE-TO-GATE (A TRIBUTE)

January 29, 2022

BACKSTAGE PASS: After I wrote *"Traveling Gate-to-Gate"*, an idea came to mind; I decided to take that initial post and convert it into a personalized tribute to some brothers who have played a significant role in my masonic journey. I have now decided to go even further and reprint it here, updating it as well, to pay tribute to other brothers who have mentored and influenced me as I have traveled my path. So, this post is not only edited for readability and grammar, but it has also been updated with the names of close and departed brothers whom I respect and miss dearly.

**

I'm moving a blog post from my website here. Although I don't often cross-post from the website to this forum, there may be an educational value to this. I've spent the day drafting a tribute to a brother. He is the fourth brother and companion I know that has passed in seven weeks - two from the lodge where I currently preside, one from one of my other lodges, and one from a York Rite chapter and council that is close to mine. The passing of these four inspiring brothers is weighing on me, and perhaps sharing this post will ease my mind. I hope you find some value in the following words. The post regards the allegorical lesson of the candidates' appearance at the West Gate.

I like to say that as masons, we travel on a journey from gate to gate. We all start at the same "west gate", metaphorically speaking, and then travel our own, individual paths on our way to the Pearly Gate. We start on the level and follow our interests and inclinations as we move through our individual lives, making our own decisions and learning our own lessons along the way, hoping again to find ourselves at that common, ultimate destination - that next and final glorious gate.

As we travel, masonry occasionally forces us to confront our mortality and ponder the immortality of our souls. It provides us with "waypoints" where we pause and ponder our present path and our ultimate destination. A brother may tell us of the passing of another brother, and we so gather in his memory to provide his Masonic graveside rites. Yes, we are seeing our brother off as he is accepted and passes through a new gate, the Pearly Gate of the Celestial Lodge above, for his next journey, but we should also be reminded of our own mortality at the same time in this solemn moment of reflection.

It is in these moments, and moments similar to these, for friends who are not masons, that we must consider our fitness, our readiness to approach and ultimately enter that next great gate. We once waited anxiously outside the Masonic West Gate; we waited to be found worthy and to be found well-qualified to enter. And our journeys will eventually take each of us to that ultimate and magnificent gate, where we will wait again to be judged on our worthiness and qualification to enter.

Will we have used our time and our travels wisely? Have we taken the opportunities along our paths to qualify ourselves for our final examination and ultimate passage through the Pearly Gate? Or have we instead failed to learn from our previous experience at the west gate of masonry? I believe this early Masonic lesson was an allegorical representation of our journey to the Pearly Gates, where, after a life fully lived, we are to be examined and – hopefully – judged worthy to pass through. In my mind, this was our preparatory lesson in masonry, teaching us that our road will one day lead us to the place and moment of ultimate judgment, and pointing us to the true beginning of a journey that may qualify us to enter that Celestial Lodge. It taught us that our own free will brings us to that Masonic west gate, and it will also be our own free will that leads us along the path of our journey to the Pearly Gate, where we will next and finally be judged.

We craved and heard the words "...*let him be received*..." at the west gate. Have we since used our journeys not merely as an adventure or, alternatively, as a life that must be endured, but rather as our path and means to prepare ourselves properly to ensure the next time we find ourselves at a gate, we hear the blessed words "...*well done, my good and faithful servant*"?

My brother, the faithful practice of masonry makes it easy to remember and occasionally ponder the purpose of our journey. When you are struggling, when you are considering a moral question of right and wrong, simply remind yourself that as a mason, you are traveling from "gate to gate".

S&F

Bro. Bill

In personal tribute to these departed brothers – you are *not* forgotten:

William Lee (Bill) Honderd who passed January 27

Jim Wheeler who passed on January 21

Embress A. (Andy) Hentschel who passed on December 31

Lewis Briley who passed on December 23

((Added in no particular order after I originally published this post))

William Norman (Norm) Ball – Somerset Masonic Lodge No. 1205

Glenn Barnhart – Somerset Masonic Lodge No. 1205

Harold Jacobs – Somerset Masonic Lodge No. 1205

Bobby Harold Jackson – Helotes Masonic Lodge No. 1429

Charlie Edward Whetstone – Helotes Masonic Lodge No. 1429/Valley-Hi Lodge No. 1407

William Joseph (Bill) Denk – Helotes Masonic Lodge No. 1429

Neil Grant Winslow – Valley-Hi Masonic Lodge No. 1407

Lawrence J. (Larry) Busby – Helotes Masonic Lodge No. 1429

James Noel (Jim) Higdon – Alamo Masonic Lodge No. 44

Timothy Malvin (Tim) Long – Valley-Hi Masonic Lodge No. 1407

Gary P. Dudley – Valley-Hi Masonic Lodge No. 1407

Joe Valenzuela – Helotes Masonic Lodge No. 1429

Robert (Bob) Cox – Alamo Masonic Lodge No. 44

Douglas (Doug) Collins – Lodge unknown

Larry Busby – Helotes Masonic Lodge No. 1429

WAIT... MASONRY EXPECTS ME TO DO MATH?

February 24, 2025

BACKSTAGE PASS: Not much going on behind the scenes with this one; it pretty much speaks for itself. I was really just answering a question that I have been asking myself all of my life – "*how does God reveal his plan for man*"? When I think about it, perhaps that is the exact same question I have also asked myself about this craft called masonry – "*how does masonry and its beautiful lessons manifest in a man's life and how would he recognize it*"?

⁑

I'm sure that at some point in your masonic journey, you've come across the term "*improve myself in masonry*" or something very close to that, but have you stopped to really think and really consider what that means? As my imaginary friend and guide, Noah Lewis, has discovered, there are hints and clues available to us everywhere, waiting patiently for our eyes to discover and our minds to conceive them. This is true within the bounds of our operative and speculative lodges, and it is true without the lodge as we walk the streets of our neighborhoods and experience life as it unfolds around us. The trick, or perhaps the actual *goal* of masonry, is to teach us to recognize and interpret those clues!

When it comes to the idea of improving oneself in masonry, we are provided with a fairly solid clue very early in our budding masonic journeys; see if these two passages sound familiar to you:

"The study of the liberal arts and sciences, that valuable branch of education which tends so effectually to polish and adorn the mind, is earnestly recommended to your careful consideration; especially the science of Geometry, which is established as the basis of our art.

"Geometry, or Masonry (originally synonymous terms), being of divine and moral nature, is enriched with the most useful knowledge; while it proves the wonderful properties of nature, it demonstrates the more important truths of morality."

Math, you ask; masonry wants me to do math? In a fashion, yes, but that is not the point. Masonry encourages each of us to "improve ourselves in masonry," and, as the passage states, there was a time when geometry and masonry were understood to be synonymous. What are we to make of this? What is this mysterious lesson that this clue alludes to?

Enough of my tease, here is my interpretation and my understanding of this instructive hint; it is through the study of the liberal arts and sciences that man might divine the information and lessons that God intends for man; if we are to become closer to our God and understand the nature of our relationship with him, we must understand the lessons he designed and provides for us.

The Grand Architect provides his designs for man and the universe through his trestle board, which we recognize as the seven liberal arts and sciences. The knowledge intended for man was preserved and passed to us by way of these lessons. It empowers us to make sense of His gifts and His wonders – the centrality of the Sun and its life-giving light, the movement of the stars in the sky and their capacity to guide both the adventurous and the lost across unexplored seas and lands. We can discover the way to properly design and shape the right angles, horizontals, and perpendiculars necessary to build our living temples in a way that is pleasing to Him.

Most of us are familiar with Euclid's Forty-Seventh Proposition, but some jurisdictions place more emphasis on this important concept than others. We know that the proposition itself was a Pythagorean equation, and we would typically learn of it and use it in geometry, but who was this *Euclid* character? Euclid, it turns out, was an ancient Greek mathematician who lived around 300 BCE in Alexandria, Egypt. Euclid came to be known as the *"Father of Geometry"* and is widely credited for the origin of the titles *"Master"* and *"Fellow"* – terms that are certainly familiar within our craft! Euclid applied the title *"master"* to those who were expert in their work and charged with <u>teaching the discipline</u> and organizing the collective knowledge of geometry (also known as *"masonry"*, remember?). The term *"fellow"* was applied to those who were part of a guild or academic society, and were those craftsmen who had advanced in their work beyond the apprentice skill level. Just a little tidbit to ponder next time you see a masonic application of the symbol representing the Pythagorean Forty-Seventh Proposition of Euclid; perhaps you might pause to consider it and the centrality of geometry itself to our craft! The more we learn and know of the arts and sciences, the more we learn and know of our craft – *the more we improve ourselves in our craft*!

Grammar, Rhetoric, Logic, Arithmetic, Geometry, Music, and Astronomy – these are the seven liberal arts and sciences. This mystic trestle board provides us insight into the mind of the Grand Architect and His ultimate plan for us. This truth was shared with us when we received our first three degrees, but many of us may have missed it in the blizzard of new words, signs, and symbols; indeed, it was my protagonist, Noah Lewis, and his fictional quest that eventually led *me* along my path to this crucial light.

As I weigh the meaning of this clue and its value and place within the context of my own journey, I also wonder why we don't seem to place enough emphasis on this lesson during our crucial, early years in the craft.

"The study of the liberal arts and sciences, that valuable branch of education which tends so effectually to polish and adorn the mind, is earnestly recommended to your careful consideration; especially the science of <u>Geometry, which is established as the basis of our art</u>."

Our ritual reveals these arts and sciences as the foundation of the mysteries that have evolved through the ages to become our beloved craft, and it bids each of us to improve ourselves in each of them. We circumambulate on a path that reveals the ecliptic as we trace the Sun on its daily path. We mimic right angles, horizontals, and perpendiculars in our steps as we approach the light. We acknowledge the summer solstice when we place our new cornerstones and our new masons in the northeast corner in homage to the rise of the Sun in the northeastern sky on that longest day of the year. It is clear that our rituals – *and therefore our mysteries* – exemplify these renowned arts and sciences, giving life to the knowledge that God has shared with humanity. Yet, I'm not sure we impress this truth on the minds or in the hearts of our newest brothers who would undoubtedly benefit from this ray of light that might illuminate the path of their nascent masonic journey. My brethren, as you go about your lives, don't forget to take some time and make some efforts to improve your knowledge of the seven liberal arts and sciences and, at the same time, uncover even more of the clues from the Grand Architect of the Universe that await you as you travel along your pathway!

I am sure some will disagree with the thoughts I've shared here and that's okay – our masonic journey is what *we* make of it, and we cannot expect others to live our truths – my only goal is to share some of my journey for your consideration and evaluation to use – *or not* – as you see fit.

My brethren, thank you for this moment of your time, and I bid you peace and harmony in your travels!

~BroBill

A Mason's Journey

ABOUT THE AUTHOR

Brother William (Bill) Boyd is a two-time Master of Valley-Hi Lodge No. 1407 AF&AM in San Antonio, Texas, which is chartered by and labors under the jurisdiction of the Most Worshipful Grand Lodge of Texas AF&AM. He was born in Washington, District of Columbia, and lived much of his life in Prince George's County in Maryland. In 1978, he joined the U.S. Air Force and left home, ultimately retiring from the service in 1998 in San Antonio.

It was in 1997 that he finally began a journey that followed in his father's footsteps to the West Gate, seeking initiation into Freemasonry. He knocked at the door of Somerset Lodge No. 1205 AF&AM in Somerset, Texas, and there completed his first three degrees when he was raised to the sublime degree of master mason in January 1999. In the subsequent time, he has presided over the Helotes York Rite in the Chapter and in the Council, as well as the San Antonio Allied Masonic Degrees Council No. 261 and the Texian York Rite College No. 60, both in San Antonio. In 2017, Bro. Boyd served as the District Deputy Grand Master for Masonic District No. 39-A of the Most Worshipful Grand Lodge of Texas AF&AM and as District Deputy Grand High Priest for Capitular District No. 23 (at that time) of the Most Excellent Grand Royal Arch Chapter of Texas.

Brother Boyd eventually turned some of his attention to writing. He began producing articles and papers that shared his thoughts and analysis on the craft, symbolism, and the state of the Masonic fraternity. He first created a group in social media (FaceBook) – "*BroBill's Masonic Education*" – as a vehicle to share educational and historical tidbits on masonry, and went on later that year to create and publish his website "*A Mason's Journey*" (www.amasonsjourney.com) where he publishes a blog and most of his articles and papers. In late 2021, he published his first book, "Noah's Quest: Trial at the Gate," which began a five-book series about the trials and personal quest of fictional Brother Noah Lewis. He has now completed the "*Noah's Quest*" fictional series and the first book in the sequel series "Noah's Legacy," where his focus now lies. He has published two non-fiction works: "*Guard Well Our Craft*" and "*In and About the Lodge*"; all seven of Brother Boyd's books have been published by Perfect Ashlar Publishing and are available on Amazon.

Brother Bill Boyd is the son of Brother Robert H. Boyd, a Maryland mason who served as master of his lodge, Chillum Castle Lodge No. 186, A.F. & A.M., in Chillum, Maryland, in 1958 before ultimately becoming the secretary of his lodge in 1959, where he served until the time he passed in 1965.

A NOTE TO THE READER

Thank you for purchasing and reading my book! I hope that this book has inspired you and has become a valuable addition to your Masonic library. If you have enjoyed this book, please consider leaving an honest review on your favorite online bookstore website.

As a special thank you for reading this book, please visit www.perfectashlarpublishing.com to access free content and stay up to date with our latest news.

OTHER BOOKS BY
PERFECT ASHLAR PUBLISHING

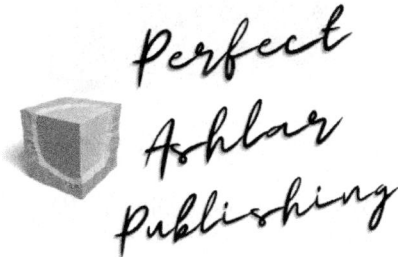

Check out these Masonic books from Perfect Ashlar Publishing.

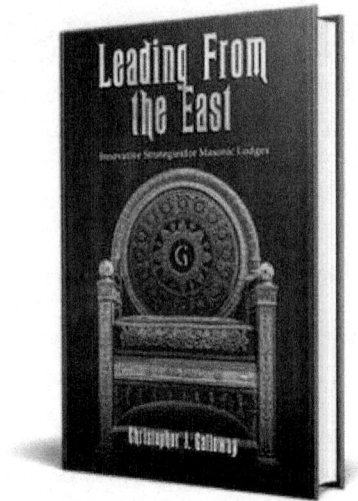

Leading from the East: Innovative Strategies for Masonic Lodges

By Christophor Galloway, PM

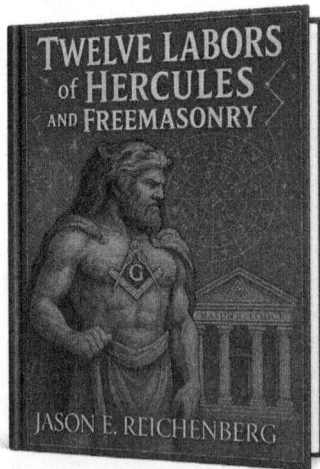

Twelve Labors of Hercules and Freemasonry

By Jason E. Reichenberg, PM

The Profound Pontifications of Big John Deacon, Freemason Extraordinaire

Volume I – IV

By James "Chris" Williams IV, PM

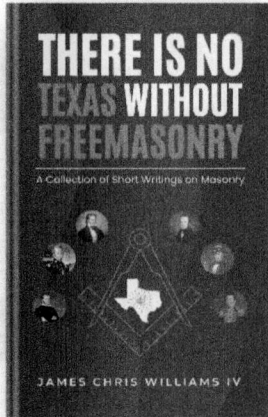

There is No Texas Without Freemasonry: A Collection of Short Writings on Masonry

By James "Chris" Williams IV, PM

Light Reflections: Philosophical Thoughts and Observations of a Texas Freemason

By Bradley E. Kohanke, PM

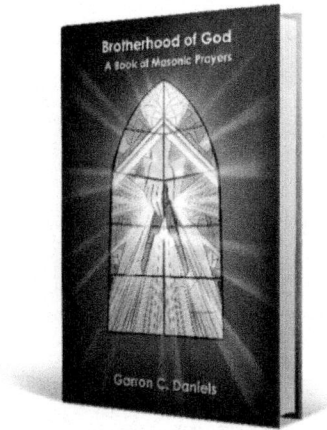

Brotherhood of God:

A Book of Masonic Prayers

By Garron C. Daniels

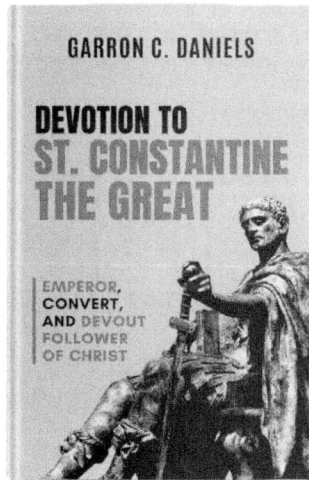

Devotion To St. Constantine the Great:

Emperor, Convert, and Devout Follower of Christ

By Garron C. Daniels

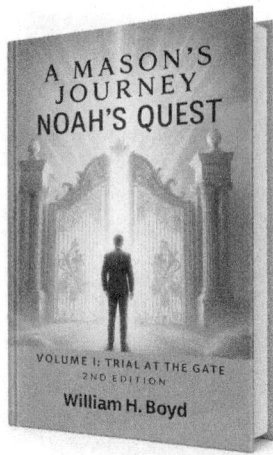

A Masons Journey – Noah's Quest:

Volume I: Trial at the Gate

By William H. Boyd

A Masons Journey – Noah's Quest:

Volume II: Eternal Awakening

By William H. Boyd

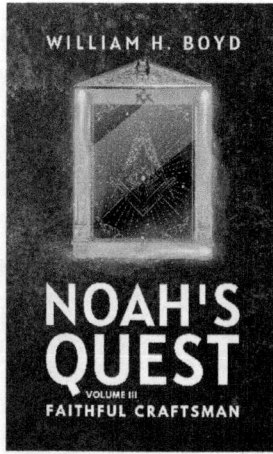

A Masons Journey – Noah's Quest:

Volume III: Faithful Craftsman

By William H. Boyd

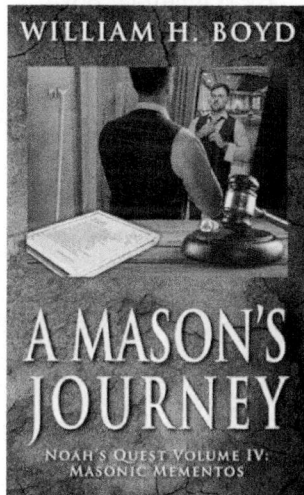

A Masons Journey – Noah's Quest:

Volume IV: Masonic Mementos

By William H. Boyd

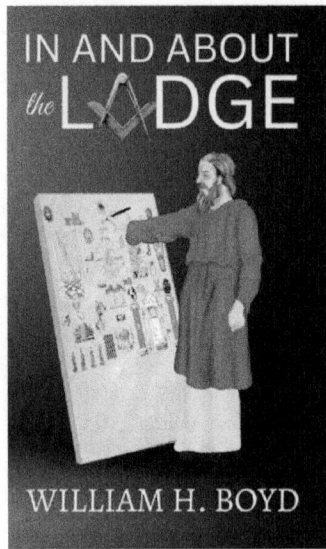

In and About the Lodge

By William H. Boyd

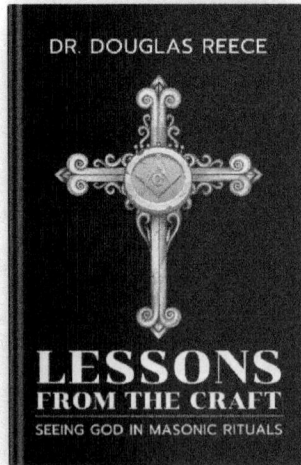

Lessons From the Craft: Seeing God in Masonic Rituals

By Dr. Douglas Reece

DR. DOUGLAS REECE

LESSONS
FROM THE RITE
OF ADOPTION
SEEING GOD IN MASONIC RITUALS

Lessons From the Rite of Adoption: Seeing God in Masonic Rituals

By Dr. Douglas Reece

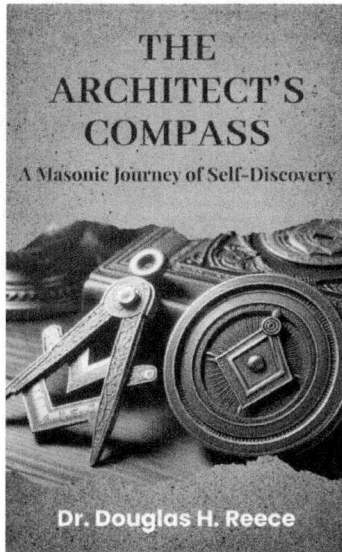

The Architect's Compass: A Masonic Journey of Self-Discovery

By Dr. Douglas Reece

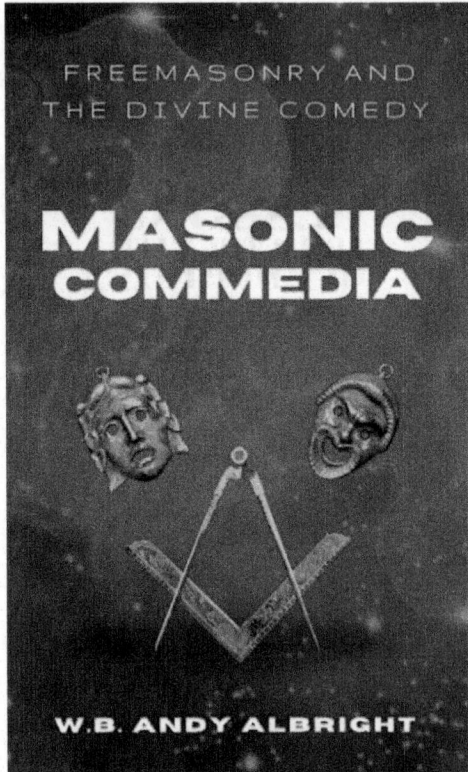

Freemasonry and the Divine Comedy

Masonic Commedia

By W.B. Andy Albright

Share Freemasonry with Future Generations with These Children's Books

By Christophor J. Galloway

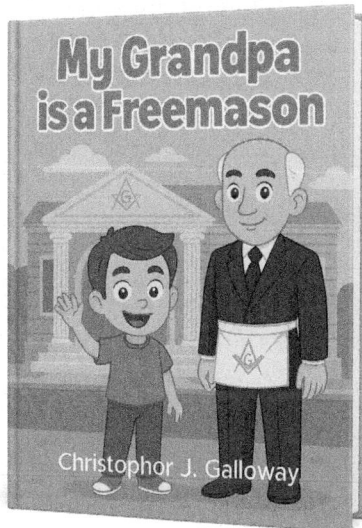

Printed in Dunstable, United Kingdom